THE CONFESSIONS OF
BLESSED ALONSO DE OROZCO

THE AUGUSTINIAN SERIES

VOLUME 23

The
Confessions
of
Blessed Alonso de Orozco

Translated by
Matthew J. O'Connell

Edited by
John E. Rotelle, O.S.A.

AUGUSTINIAN PRESS
1991

Nihil Obstat: James McGrath
  Censor Librorum

Imprimatur: Anthony J. Bevilacqua
  Archbishop of Philadelphia

The introduction and notes of Arturo Llin Cháfer were translated into English by Audrey Fellowes; the *Confesiones* and notes were translated by Matthew J. O'Connell.

Translation of the *Confesiones del Beato Alonso de Orozco*, Manila 1882.

Cover illustration: Fray Alonso de Orozco, the writer.

Library of Congress Catalog Card Number: 91-70265
ISBN: 0-941491-26-9 (paper)
        0-941491-46-3 (cloth)
        0-941491-09-9 (series)

AUGUSTINIAN PRESS
P.O. Box 476
Villanova, PA 19085

Printed in the United States of America

Contents

The Confessions
of Blessed Alonso de Orozco

Book I

Book II

Book III

Foreword

The English translation of the *Confesiones del Beato Alonso de Orozco* is based on the 1882 edition which was printed in Manila, the Philippines.

Fray Alonso completed the *Confesiones* in 1580; he completed the *Memorial* in 1589-1590. The first printed edition of the *Confesiones* appeared in 1601, in Valladolid, Spain, through the initiative of Fray Augustín Antolinez, O.S.A., prior provincial at the time. Fray Juan de Critiana, O.S.A., directed the work. At the end of the third book of the *Confesiones* the *Memorial* of favors and graces received were added, eight in all.

A second edition of the *Confesiones*, orchestrated by Fray Juan de Herrera, postulator of Alonso's cause for beatification, was printed in Madrid in 1620. To this addition was added notes by Fray Basilio Ponce de Léon and Alonso's funeral oration by Fray Pedro Manrique.

Other editions followed — all based on the original 1601 edition which was printed from the original manuscript which Fray Alonso de Orozco wrote: Zaragoza, 1678; Madrid, 1730; Manila, 1881. In 1624 and 1696 there appeared editions in Italian; in 1643 a edition appeared in French.

In 1991, to commemorate the 400th anniversary of Blessed Alonso de Orozco's death, this first edition in English appears. The editor thanks Balbino Rano, O.S.A., for the copy of the 1881 manuscript. Gratitude must be expressed to Joseph A. Grifferty, O.S.A., and to Scott Ness, O.S.A., for their preliminary work in translation, and to Matthew O'Connell, the translator. I am grateful to Father Arturo Llin Cháfer for his introduction.

A special note of thanks to Fray Luciano Rubio, O.S.A., who has shared with me his edition (1990) of the *Confesiones* in which he provides information concerning the various editions and in-depth research on Blessed Alonso's works.

John E. Rotelle, O.S.A.

Introduction

A publication of Blessed Alonso de Orozco is an opportunity to make known "one of the most outstanding writers of devotional literature in the Spanish Golden Age."[1]

In his own time he made himself known by his sermons and the books on spirituality which he wrote, in the purest Spanish, covering the various problems encountered in Christian life. In his works he teaches the science of prayer. He is a catechist who reflects profoundly on the mystery and ministry of God's word. He tries to instruct Christians and help them to be truly Christian. He does so with forceful argument and doctrinal richness, with touching enthusiasm, in clear spontaneous language, sonorous, refined, and pure.

First Years in the Religious Life

Alonso de Orozco belongs to the Spanish Golden Age, in which there arose an incomparable pleiad of devout men who made a notable impression on the Church of those days, with universal implications.

As an Augustinian friar Orozco witnessed the renascence of the Augustinian Order in Spain, which contributed such eminent figures to the Spanish Church of the sixteenth century as Dionisio Vázquez (3 June 1479-1 August 1539), preacher and biblical scholar, forerunner of the ascetical-mystical flowering of the sixteenth century;[2] Alfonso de Córdoba (d. 4 October 1541), philosopher, professor of nominalism in Alcalá de Henares and Salamanca;[3] Saint Thomas of Villanova (1486-September 1555), Augustinian provincial in Andalusia and Castilla, visitor general, famous preacher, archbishop of Valencia;[4] Luis de Alarcón (1490-1550), ascetical-mystical writer;[5] Luis de Montoya (15 May 1497-7 September 1571), reformer of the Augustinians in Portugal, ascetical-mystical writer;[6] Juan de Muñatones (d. 15 April 1571), preacher to the Emperor Charles V, bishop of Segorbe, participant in the

Council of Trent;[7] Pedro de Uceda (1523-1586), theologian, rector of the University of Alcalá de Henares;[8] Pedro Malón de Chaide (1530-1 September 1589), ascetic writer, professor at the universities of Huesca and Saragossa;[9] Luis de Léon (1527-27 August 1591), poet, philosopher, theologian, biblical scholar, and mystic.[10]

The Augustinian Order participated in the heightened spiritual climate created by the recent reform of its monasteries. At the special chapter held at Toledo in 1507, the Augustinian province of Castilla was totally incorporated with all its monasteries in the congregation of the observance.[11] The reform of the Spanish Augustinians had begun in 1431, with Friar Juan de Alarcón, culminating in 1438 with the creation of the observance.[12] Gradually the reform movement of the Augustinian observance began to assert itself, and in the year 1451 the monastery of Saint Augustine at Salamanca was incorporated in the observant congregation.[13]

Salamanca

Alonso de Orozco was born in Oropesa (Toledo) on 1 October 1500,[14] and we meet him at the age of fourteen already studying the arts at the University of Salamanca. There he was to observe the spiritual atmosphere pervading the Augustinian monastery at Salamanca, where the cloisters were still redolent with the virtues of Saint Juan de Sahagún (1430-11 June 1479).[15]

He witnessed the entry of Tomas García (the future Saint Thomas of Villanova) into that monastery as a member of the Order on 21 November 1516,[16] his later profession,[17] ordination as priest,[18] and ministerial activities.[19]

The monastery of Salamanca had always been a *studium generale* (major house of studies) of the Augustinian Order.[20] The provincial chapter of Castilla, held at Arenas de San Pedro (Avila) on 30 May 1511, gives definite orders for the "continual" study of "arts and theology" in the monastery of

Salamanca, "and nominates Father Alfonso de Cordóba as director of studies."[21]

It is not surprising that Thomas of Villanova, with the cultural equipment he brought to religion, was invited to impart his theological learning:

> In his capacity as priest . . . they sent him to lecture on scholastic theology in the monastery of our father Saint Augustine at Salamanca . . . with the result that he lectured to the religious of his own house and also to a great many students who came from the university to listen to the Master of the Sentences, who always followed and had made his own the teaching of the Angelic Doctor, Saint Thomas Aquinas.[22]

To this ministry he was soon obliged to add others. His superiors quickly called upon him to devote himself to preaching the word of God:

> He began to devote himself to the sacred task of preaching, with such speed that even at the beginning he gave the clearest proof of a most ardent spirit toward God, and an admirable concern for religion and divine honor and the spiritual welfare of his fellow beings.[23]

The effect of his activities was to produce the beginning of a Christian renewal, not only in the town of Tormes, but in all the villages belonging to its district. No wonder, since the whole population went to hear him:

> And there was no one who heard him without being changed, moved, and inspired by the love of God. They went away from his sermons as if stunned, gazing at each other, amazed at seeing the power with which he taught, . . . since he moved them to true compunction and tears, and to hope and inward joy.[24]

It did not take long to become aware of the spiritual renewal that accompanied his ministerial activities. In his *Historia del Convento de san Agustin de Salamanca* Tomás de Herrera describes it as an event which left its mark for some time on the local community:

His preaching found its way so deeply into the hearts of
the people. . . . He inspired affection principally in the
scholastics, men dedicated to learning, who filled that
large University; . . . he taught them to scorn the adulation
of the present and long for the good things of the world to
come, and made the divine cause so attractive to them that
not only the monasteries of that town . . . but even the
religious houses of the surrounding villages . . . were hardly
enough to admit all who begged for entrance.

During the years in which Saint Thomas of Villanova lived
at Salamanca, as prior 1519-1521 and 1523-1525, the same
renewal observed in that town and its district was seen in a
splendid vocational flowering in the Augustinian monastery.
Among those who entered the monastery, attracted by the
ministry of Saint Thomas of Villanova, was Alonso de Orozco,
who together with his brother Francisco[25] began the novitiate
on 8 June 1522.[26]

During the canonical year of religious training his master
was Luis de Montoya,[27] a colleague of Saint Thomas in the
same monastery. "His teaching agrees in its principles and
orientation with that of Saint Thomas of Villanova, as the
teaching of both proceeds from the same traditional sources
and both show intense and practical devotion to Christ and
his holy Mother."[28]

Luis de Montoya was able to harmonize love and gentleness
with austere asceticism, and at the invitation of Saint Thomas
of Villanova was able to unite "action and contemplation in
his life, and in the practice of this incorporate the new teachings
of his great friend Saint Ignatius Loyola."[29]

So equipped it is easy to understand how the master set
about shaping the spirit of the young Alonso de Orozco, who
only longed for continuous progress on the road of Christian
perfection. On 9 June 1523, he made his religious profession
under the guidance of the prior of the monastery, Saint

Thomas of Villanova.[30] Shortly afterward he was ordained a priest. Conscious of the importance of the priesthood, he would try to make himself worthy of it by the sanctity of a blameless life.[31] From the beginning of his priesthood the superiors of the Order appointed him to preach. It was to be the primary task to which he would preferably devote himself throughout his long life.

Administrative Offices

In the year 1525 the monastery of Our Lady of Grace was founded in the small town of Medina del Campo, and the following year Father Luis de Montoya was appointed prior.[32] Among the friars who accompanied him when he left Salamanca to take up this office was Blessed Alonso de Orozco, who would continue to share his master's teaching.

In 1637 Orozco was appointed prior of the monastery of Saint Augustine at Soria,[33] where the friars directed a college of the arts for lay people, teaching grammar, philosophy, and moral theology, whose patron was Our Lady of Grace. There he completed his training in the apostolate, and with the experience he was continually acquiring he began to outline the spiritual teaching which he would formulate in his books.

In 1539 Father Montoya gave up the priorship of Medina del Campo and was appointed as visitor and reformer of the Augustinian province of Portugal, where he remained until his death in Lisbon on 7 September 1569.[34] The year following the departure of Montoya from Medina, Alonso de Orozco was appointed superior of this monastery.[35] On 9 November 1540 he attended the provincial chapter at Dueñas, where in the presence of the prior general, Jerome Seripando,[36] the members discussed the advisability of uniting the two provinces of Andalusia and Castilla in a single province for the better care of the houses and the friars. Given the large area of the new province it was agreed to divide it into "three visitations": Salamanca, Toledo, and Seville. Father Orozco was appointed provincial definitor.[37]

From 1542 till November 1544 Orozco was acting prior at the Augustinian monastery in Seville. Founded in 1248 by King Ferdinand III the Saint, the richness of the paintings in the church and cloister made it an artistic monument. It was still remembered that Saint Thomas of Villanova had passed through this monastery during his provincialate in Andalusia in the years 1527-1529.[38] It was in this house that Alonso de Orozco twice saw the Virgin Mary in dreams, encouraging him to write, and he wrote his first book, *Garden of Prayer and Mountain of Contemplation.*[39]

From Seville in 1544 he went to be prior of the monastery in Granada. He held this office simultaneously with that of visitor of Andalusia.[40] In 1547, free of all duties, he asked to be allowed to go to the missions in New Spain, where the Augustinians had charge of a flourishing mission. For a year he waited in vain in Gomera (Canary Islands) for a boat to take him to the American mainland.[41]

It seems that when he returned to Spain it was to the monastery in Seville, where once more the Virgin honored him with another vision, "to comfort him in the troubles and trials he was enduring."[42]

Preacher at the Imperial Court

Blessed Alonso de Orozco was appointed prior of the monastery of Saint Augustine in Valladolid, one of the best in Castilla, where there was a university. The admirable activities he displayed in this city, at that time occasionally the residence of the imperial court, came to the notice of the Emperor Charles V, who wished to avail himself of his advice and preaching.[43] On 13 March 1554, the Emperor appointed him royal preacher.[44]

In 1556 Alonso de Orozco founded in Talavera de la Reina the monastery of Our Lady of Peace, where the first community of discalced Augustinians was formed, and that house was the first in which the Recollects established the foundations of their congregation on 10 October 1589.[45] The court was transferred to Madrid in 1560 and Orozco also had to move in order to continue his priestly ministry with the Emperor, his family, and the imperial court.[46] He took up residence in the monastery of San Felipe del Real. This monastery was founded by Saint Thomas of Villanova in 1544, and was named San Felipe to mark the generosity shown by King Philip II at its foundation. Saint Thomas was unable to satisfy his wish to be a friar there himself, as in the same year he became Archbishop of Valencia, but Orozco lived in that house for many years, setting an example of humility, with no ecclesiastical preferment, and renouncing whatever privilege his office of royal preacher might have conferred on him.

He illuminated all with his words, directed all with his advice, but above all he instructed them with his holy life, which was the best sermon he could have preached. What he received for his office as royal preacher he gave to the poor, so a great number of people were helped by his proverbial generosity.[47]

Among those he directed at the court was Maria de Córdoba y Aragón, daughter of Alvaro de Córdoba, master of the horse to King Philip II, and Maria de Aragón, lady-in-waiting to queen Anne of Austria. Her first confessor was Father Juan de Vega, but at his death in 1580[48] she chose Alonso de Orozco as her spiritual director, showing that she had a special veneration for the Augustinian Order.

When she founded the monastery and college of the Incarnation for the study of theology she entrusted it to the Augustinians.[49] It was already arranged in 1588 that a religious community was to take possession of that house, and that Orozco would be its rector. But this project was only realized two years later.

Together with two other friars Father Orozco began living, in a rather provisional manner, in this new foundation on 3 April 1591. But on 10 August he fell seriously ill, and died in sanctity on 19 September 1591 at the age of 91.

He was buried in the chapel of that college.[50] After various moves, when only the college of the Dulce Nombre de Jesús at Valladolid was left, thanks to the disentailment laws of 1835, his remains were taken to this college.

He was beatified by Pope Leo XIII on 15 January 1882. The Augustinian Order celebrates his liturgical feast on 19 September.

Conclusion

This biographical sketch of Blessed Alonso de Orozco presents us with the itinerary of his religious life. It was abundantly rich in the kind of experience that would enable him to convey in his writings the teaching with which he was to illuminate Christians, who turned to him for instruction in order to receive light and orientation on their own way through life. There was no aspect of ecclesial life that escaped Orozco's careful attention. In this way, throughout his ministry, he tried to impress the gospel on all through is own witness.

Trainer of friars and missionaries, famous preacher of God's word at the imperial court and in the Christian community, director of chosen souls whom he guided along the path of sanctity, counselor to the rulers of Church and society, he was always able to expound the criteria and principles adequate to introduce the new paths which the Church and society of his time required, and which he made clear in his own ecclesial dedication to all who came to him for pastoral guidance.

Arturo Llin Cháfer

NOTES

1. I. Rodriguez, *Ascéticos y místicos agustinos españoles del siglo XVI: Corrientes espirituales en la España del siglo XVI* (Barcelona, 1963) 327.

2. A. Manrique: *Diccionario de historia eclesiástica de España*, edited by Q. Aldea and others (Madrid, 1972) vol. 4, 2715-2716.

3. E.D. Carretero, *ibid.*, vol. 1, 618-619.

4. A. Iturbe, *ibid.*, vol. 4, 2763-2765.

5. A. Manrique, *ibid.*, vol. 1, 29.

6. I. Rodriguez, *Ascéticos y místicos agustinos españoles del siglo XVI, op. cit.*, 323-326.

7. T. de Herrera, *Historia del convento de San Agustin de Salamanca* (Madrid, 1652) 312-315.

8. E.D. Carretero, *Diccionario de historia eclesiástica de España*, vol. 4, 2603-2604.

9. A. Espada, *op. cit.*, vol. 2, 1405-1406.

10. E.D. Carretero, *op. cit.*, vol. 2, 1286-1288.

11. L. Alvarez, "La 'Observancia' agustiniana de Castilla en el siglo XV: Corrientes espirituales, organización y regimen de vida," *Revista Agustiniana de Espiritualidad* 43-44 (1973) 96-105; *ibid.*, "Fusión de la Provincia Agustiniana de Castilla con la congregación homónima, culminando la Reforma Observante," *Revista Agustiniana de Espiritualidad* 39 (1971) 371-405.

12. With the permission of Father Agustín Romaño, Prior General of the Augustinians, "the Venerable Father Friar Juan de Alarcón founded the Monastery of the Saints, which was the first in which the Observance was instituted; this was possibly in the same year, 1431, in which on 17 April the same Prior General also appointed him in the first place to be President and Vicar General of the Provincial Chapter, which was due to be held in Dueñas at Pentecost in 1432," T. de Herrera, *op. cit.*, 16. To increase the number of foundations Father Alarcón "requested the Prior General, Gerard of Rimini, to establish a Congregation of the Observance separate from and independent of the Province. His devout wish found favor with the Prior General Gerard of Rimini, who granted his request on 7 June 1438 while he was at Ferrara," T. de Herrera, *op. cit.*, 27. In the Augustinian Provincial archives of Castilla, in Madrid, can be found the decree of the Prior General, Gerard of Rimini, regulating the life of the observance (11 November 1438), in the section for unnumbered documents. Also to be found in the same archives is the bull of confirmation from Pope Eugene IV.

13.   Vicar General Father Juan de Montelongo was elected to the chapter of the congregation in 1451, and it was "in his time" that "the monastery of Saint Augustine was incorporated into the Congregation of the Observance in the year 1451," T. de Herrera, *op. cit.*, 32; M. Andres, "Reforma y estudio de la teología entre los agustinos reformados españoles," *Anthologica annua* 4 (1956) 439-462.

14.   See *Confessions of Blessed Alfonso de Orozco*, page 35.

15.   San Juan de Sahagún, born about the year 1430, in Sahagún, in the province of Léon. "While he was still a student and not yet a priest he was granted a benefice in the town of Cordonillos." "The bishop of Burgos, Alonso de Cartagena, ordained him priest. He devoted himself to preaching the word of God. He entered the monastery of Saint Augustine (at Salamanca) and after probation took his vows on 28 August 1464." "He excelled as a peacemaker between the factions which divided the city of Salamanca, owing to the rivalries between the Monroyes and Manzanos." "He was prior of the monastery at Salamanca in 1471 and 1477." "Because of the ardor of his preaching . . . he was given the title of Apostle of Salamanca . . . he died in the peace of the Lord on 11 June 1479," C. de Santiago Vela, *Ensayo de una biblioteca Iberoaméricana de la orden de San Agustin* (Madrid - El Escorial, 1913-1931) volume 7, 7-24.

16.   M. Salon, *Libros de los grandes y singularísimos ejemplos que dejó de si en todo genero de santidad y virtud . . . el Ilustrisimo y Reverendisimo Sr. D. Fray Thomás de Villanueva* (Valencia, 1620) 17.

17.   "He took his vows in the monastery (of Saint Augustine at Salamanca) on Saint Catherine's day 25 November 1517, because that is what this witness has seen in an old book registering the professions of the sons of the said monastery . . ." Fr. Diego de Guevara, Archives.

18.   M. Salon, *op. cit.*, 23; B. Rano, "Notas críticas sobre los 57 años primeros de santo Tomás de Villanueva," *La Ciudad de Dios* 171 (1958) 674.

19.   M. Salon, *op. cit.*, 27, 75.

20.   T. de Herrera, *op. cit.*, 230.

21.   E.D. Carretero, "La escuela teológica agustiniana de Salamanca," *La Ciudad de Dios* 169 (1956) 651.

22.   M. Salon , *op. cit.*, 27.

23.   T. de Herrera, *op. cit.*, 313.

24.   M. Salon, *op. cit.*, 30-31.

25.   Francisco, the brother of Blessed Alonso de Orozco, did not complete his novitiate, since he died young after enduring a mortal illness with great resignation.

26.   C. de Santiago Vela, *op. cit.*, vol. 7, 96-102.

27. Luis de Montoya, after completing his ecclesiastical studies in 1521, became novice master; prior of Medina del Campo (1526- 1535). He became visitor and reformer of the Augustinian province of Portugal; preceptor to King Sebastian of Portugal. He wrote some books on spiritual doctrine. J.M. de Estal, *Diccionario de historia eclesiástica de España*, vol. 3, 1736-1737.

28. D. Gutiérrez, *op. cit.*, 166.

29. *Ibid.*, 167.

30. C. Abad, "Ascetas y místicos españoles del siglo de oro," *Miscelánea de Comillas* 10 (1948) 27.

31. A. de Orozco, *Memorial del Amor Santo* (Salamanca, 1896) 415-416.

32. J. Lanteri, "Additamenta ad Crisenii Augustinianum Monasticon,": *Regista Agustiniana* 9 (1885) 244.

33. T. Camara, *Vida y escritos del Beato Alonso de Orozco* (Valladolid 1882) 78-79.

34. J.M. de Estal, *op. cit.*, 1736-1737.

35. T. Camara, *op. cit.*, 75.

36. Jerome Seripando, born at Troya de Pugia (Italy) about the year 1492/1493. In 1507 he entered the Augustinian monastery of Saint John at Carbonera, the principal town in the observantine province of the same name; he was elected prior general at the general chapter held in Naples in 1539. From 1539 to 1542 he traversed Italy, France, Spain, and Portugal visiting the monasteries of his Order.

He took part in the Council of Trent (1545-1548), collaborating in the redaction of the decree on justification. On 30 March 1554 he was nominated archbishop of Salerno, and on 26 February 1561 Pope Pius IV created him cardinal and afterward his legate at the Council of Trent. He died at Trent on 17 March 1563, and was buried in the Augustinian Church of Saint Mark in that city, H. Jedin, *Enciclopedia cattolica*, 11 (Vatican City) 389-390; *Diarium de vita sua (1531-1562): Analecta Augustiniana* 26 (1963) 1-192.

37. B. Estrada, *Los agustinos ermitaños en España hasta el siglo XIX* (Madrid, 1988) 78-79.

38. *Ibid.*, 427.

39. C. de Santiago Vela, "El Convento de Sevilla," *Archivo Agustiniana* 12 (1919) 48.

40. T. Camara, *op. cit.*, 102.

41. C. de Santiago Vela, *Ensayo de una biblioteca . . .*, vol. 7, 96-102.

42. T. Camara, *op. cit.*, 594-595.

43.   *Ibid.*, 116.

44.   *Ibid.*

45.   C. de Santiago Vela, "La provincia de Castilla en 1588," *Archivo Agustiniano* 23 (1925) 43-46.

46.   A.J. Boulovas, *El amor divino en la obra del beato Alonso de Orozco* (Madrid, 1975) 32.

47.   T. Camara, *op. cit.*, 133.

48.   J. Guijarro, "Memorias para la historia de la provincia de Castilla," *Archivo Agustiniano* 57 (1963) 6-8.

49.   C. de Santiago Vela, "El Colegio de la Encarmación de Madrid," *Archivo Agustiniano* 10 (1981) 10-11; 82-87.

50.   *Ibid.*, 12.

Biography

An Account of the Life
of the Venerable Father
Fray Alonso de Orozco

written by
Father Master Fray Hernando de Rojas
his confessor
and presented at the
process for his beatification

ur Father Alonso de Orozco was the son of very upright parents: his father was Hernando de Orozco, and his mother, a native of Oropesa, was named Maria de Mena. His father and uncles were mayors of Torico and Oropesa and of the entire lands of the Count of Oropesa. Alonso was born shortly after dark on Thursday, 16 October 1500, the eve of the feast of Saint Luke. At the first stroke of the *Ave Maria* bell his mother's birth pains began, and at the last stroke he was born. He was given the name Alonso because this had been revealed to his mother; she said that when she was reflecting on what name to give him, she heard a voice saying, "Call him Alonso."

Alonso grew up in Oropesa until he was eight, when his parents left there and transferred to Talavera; it was in the latter town that he learned to read and write. From there they moved on to Toledo, where he remained three years, serving in the main church as a singer and becoming a very skilled cantor. From there he went with his old brother Francisco to study in Salamanca; his subject was law. His brother was intending to become a monk, and when Alonso learned of this, he frequently asked him to arrange for both of them to enter the monastery. The brother objected, "It is not right that you too should become a monk: this would be a misfortune for our parents, since they have no other sons." Alonso answered, "Brother, let us save ourselves! God will see to it that our parents are comforted." As a result, both brothers entered the convent of Saint Augustine in Salamanca, but the older brother died as a novice.

Alonso's Master of Novices was Father Luis de Montoya, who later reformed the Province of Portugal, where, having lived a very holy and very religious life, he died as he had lived and was regarded as one of the blessed. Alonso's profession was received by Father Thomas of Villanova, who subsequently became the very holy Archbishop of Valencia. The young monk studied the arts and theology in Salamanca, where he also began his preaching.

Alonso was prior in many houses of the Order; these may appropriately be listed here: Soria, Medina del Campo, Valladolid, Granada, and Seville, where our Lord bestowed special favors on him. In particular, he had been greatly afflicted by scruples for thirty years and had asked God, through the intercession of his Mother Mary, to deliver him from them; one night, as he returned from Matins to his cell, he heard a loud howling of dogs and then a gentle voice saying to him, "Alonso, they are defeated and are departing." From then on, Alonso said, he lived as though he were in heaven, with great serenity and peace of conscience.

He said, too, that at that time our Lady appeared to him in the form of a very lovely young girl; with her very beautiful eyes she stole his soul from him. When telling me of the incident, he said her eyes were so beautiful that painters had never succeeded in depicting them as they really are; if he himself were a painter (he said), he thought he might be able to capture them as they truly are. Our Lady consoled him; Alonso thanked her for this mark of kindness and asked her to let him know what works he could do in gratitude for so great a favor. The sovereign Lady told him that he would perform great services for her by his writing and preaching. He continued both of these activities until the very end of his life.

He wrote countless books in Latin and Spanish. So regularly did he preach that without even being asked to do so he visited all the monasteries of nuns and all the hospitals and frequently the prisons as well, and there preached with great fervor and devotion. In addition, there were the sermons he preached at the royal palace to his Majesty the Emperor and King Philip II, whose preacher he became on 13 March 1554. When he was prior of the convent in Valladolid, Emperor Charles V showed him favor and from Brussels sent him a document now in my possession.

Many monks who resided with Alonso as superior and subject have said in my hearing that in these positions he gave a fine example to superiors and subjects respectively. Since there are many witnesses in the other convents where he resided who can tell how and in what spirit he lived and what example he gave, I shall tell only what I myself saw during the eleven or twelve months in which I was his unworthy companion in this college. He was visited here by all the princes and lords of the court and frequently by King Philip II and his son, Prince Philip, and by the Infanta, Doña Isabel. All these people loved him and venerated him as a saint. The king often sent his ministers, and especially Juan Ruiz de Velasco, with messages for Alonso, asking him to intercede with the Lord. So great was his humility that he easily avoided the vainglory to which such visits and favors might have given rise.

He neither wanted nor took steps to secure anything for himself or his cell. He swept his own cell and emptied his own pitcher. He did not want to be called "Your Paternity," and often said, when I addressed him in that way, "Father, let us not wrest the name 'Paternity' from God; let us call one another 'Charity' or 'Love,' for this name will remind us of how we ought to deal with one another." He practiced poverty to an unusual degree. It is worth noting that although he received an income once the emperor made him his preacher (as I mentioned earlier), he used this to free prisoners from jail and support some of the poor who were in jail, as well as for the regular alms which he distributed each month; to some of the poor he gave four reals, to others six, bestowing favor as need required. In like manner, he provided alms for a monastery of nuns which he established in the city of Talavera. For the poor whom he might meet each day he prepared bits of paper containing ten or twelve maravedis; he gave one of these to each comer. When I said that since so many came he should divide the alms so as to give only four or even two maravedis to everyone, he answered that he must not give a poor person an alms insufficient to buy a loaf of bread with which to stay hunger.

So great was his love for the poor that if while praying in the choir he heard a poor person in the church, he would say to me, "Father, wait for me here and take note of where we left off; our Lord will be served even by this little pause, since I am going to help a brother in need." Then he would go his cell, get a piece of paper with the four maravedis in it, and give it to the person, at the same time speaking a word of comfort to him. As a result, no one came to him in any need, spiritual or temporal, and went away uncomforted. And so many were those who came with the one or the other need that I cannot explain, except by saying I think it a miracle, how he helped so many people and gave so many alms from such a small income.

He was a man of great devotion, especially to the Blessed Sacrament. He often left his cell and went to the choir, where he remained before the Blessed Sacrament. If he saw someone enter the church, he would thank him for having come in and would tell him that by entering the Lord's presence he was doing him a favor that meant more to him than the presence of the kings of earth. As a result of his devotion, one morning, after he had prayed before the Blessed Sacrament, the Lord bestowed a consolation on him by giving him communion, as Alonso himself has written and attested. He told me of this favor in confession and bade me write it down, and then he signed it himself. (This paper is with the others which we are giving to Father Román [the postulator or procurator in charge of the beatification process].) He was most devout in his manner of saying Mass; if it happened on one or another day that because of a fever or some other indisposition the doctors told him not to say Mass, he would answer that they ought not to deprive him of the true salvation which is God and that God does no harm to anyone.

He practiced a very great abstinence and from the time when he entered religion until the time when God took him to himself he always fasted three days a week, often on bread and water. He always shared his food with the poor. His ordinary meal was a bowl of hot water with a few vegetables boiled in it. His ration of meat he always gave to the poor. He never took supper; when he grew very old and could not sleep, the doctors told him to eat supper, but even then his meal consisted only of some boiled lettuce and a few crumbs of bread.

His tunic was always of very rough serge, and he almost always wore a hairshirt. His black and white habit was of very coarse, cheap cloth. Some things — tunics, stockings, under-vests — he sewed himself. His bedding was extremely poor and rough, since for almost the whole of his life it was simply a board or some vine cuttings or a straw mattress. Most recently, while in this college, at the urging of Queen María of Aragón and on the orders of Father Provincial, he accepted having a further thin mattress; on this he lay, covered with some blankets of goats' hair or goats' skins. Whenever he did lie on his bed, he wrapped himself in a narrow bag or sack, and so accustomed was he to this that even when he fell into the final illness from which God took him, he lay thus on his bed. When I urged him to get rid of the sack from his bed, I could hardly get anywhere with him, for he told me that the purpose of the sack was to dispose him for death and burial, which was what a bed represented.

He was extremely patient in suffering and sickness, and when the pain intensified he would say, "My Lord, mercy!" His final illness was the severest, since he had a double tertian fever that lasted forty-one days; during this period they bled him often, applied cupping glasses and leeches to him, and gave him numerous syrups and purgatives and ointments. Despite all these agonies and the sickness itself, and despite his being ninety-one years old, he arose daily to say Mass for the first twenty days. His case was miraculous and virtually unheard of.

On the days when he rose from his bed, he also heard the confessions of some ladies whose usual confessor he was, and gave them communion. One day he exorcised a possessed woman and cast the demon out of her, and gave a spiritual talk to all who happened to be present. On the second twenty days, when he could not arise, he ordered me to bring him the sacrament which he then received and adored. It is to be noted that when the doctors refused to let him get up and say Mass on the grounds that he was too fatigued, he answered that the saying of Mass reduced his weakness. And indeed he undoubtedly returned to his bed in better condition and said Mass with such calm and energy that he seemed very healthy. He asked the doctors who the authorities were who claimed that the saying of Mass must be injurious. When they told him "Galen, Hippocrates, and Avicenna," he laughed at them and told them, "Pagan witnesses, of course! Don't believe them, for they are in hell!" During his illness, which was long and severe, the princes and lords of the court came to visit and be of service to him. Every day, morning and evening, the empress sent her stewards to bring the broth which she and her ladies made with their own hands. Cardinal Gaspar de Quiroga, Archbishop of Toledo, came thrice to visit him, and one of the royal doctors sent a daily report to his majesty at the Escorial on the condition of Father Alonso. María of Aragón and her sister, the Countess of Buendia, stayed throughout the forty days to nurse him. To these women and their servants and to us monks who were present the day before he departed for heaven, he preached a sermon. (The gist of this was copied down as he preached it; I have given the paper to Father Román along with the other documents.) The sermon was a summary of the man's life and of the manner of life which we ought to make our own; it urges us to practice charity, patience, humility, and the other virtues.

During the night, his last on earth, he made his confession to me; in less than half an hour he made a most complete, sensible, and exemplary confession. It is my opinion that in his ninety-one years of life he had never committed a mortal sin.

His death resembled his life in that he was born and died on a Thursday; having been born on a Thursday, he was most devoted to the Blessed Sacrament. He died on 19 September at the age of ninety-one; after his death he remained whiter than a crystal in appearance. We left his whole virginal body (for he was indeed a virgin, as he told me in confession) on display for twenty-four hours in the college chapel; all of Madrid came to see him and kiss his feet and cut pieces from his habit. They came also to his solemn burial, which was attended by all the orders and the lords of the court; the Bishop of Ciudad Rodrigo said the funeral Mass. We buried him in the cavity of the altar in the college church, because that was the place appointed by Cardinal Gaspar de Quiroga, Archbishop of Toledo. In my opinion, this decision was not his alone, but heaven's as well. It was right that this man who paid so much honor to the altar during his life should be honored by the altar in death.

I shall say nothing here of the blessings and favors which our Lord and his most holy Mother bestowed on this man in life and in death. Some of them Alonso himself describes in his *Confessions*. Others are written in his own hand on separate pieces of paper signed by him, which have been given to

Father Román. The miracles that occurred at his death and since then are well-known to all.

☐   ☐   ☐   ☐

On 23 January 1603, twelve years after the precious death of this holy man, his venerable body was transferred to the church of the College of Doña María of Aragón. It was found to be incorrupt and as intact as if it were still alive: the fingers and neck could be moved, the belly yielded to the touch, the eye sockets were unwithered, and his garment was not moth-eaten. For two hundred and ten years the precious relics were suitably deposited there, for the consolation of the sick and infirm. On 19 September 1813, they were taken to the convent of the Augustinian nuns in Madrid, known as the Convent of the Magdalenes, which Alonso himself had established. The Magdalenes guarded the relics with great respect for twelve years; then, on 23 August 1825, the remains returned to their ancient resting place in the College of Doña María of Aragón and were kept there until 1835, when they were once again placed in the Convent of the Magdalenes.

Their stay, however, was a brief one, for in that same year they were taken to the Church of Saint Sebastian in Madrid, until at the request of the Order the necessary permission was obtained from Rome to transfer them to the Philippines and the college there of the Augustinians from Valladolid (Province of the Holy Name of Jesus), where they have been piously venerated to the present day. In that same year, for our happiness and the happiness of that country, various relics of the blessed reached those islands, among them a sizable one that is venerated in the Church of Saint Augustine in the capital city.

Because the body of Venerable Alonso had been found incorrupt when its first transfer took place, Alonso's confessor, Father Rojas, asked the ecclesiastical authorities to let him initiate the appropriate proceedings; the permission was granted without delay, and the first stage toward beatification was thus taken. Later on, at the request of Father Herrera, the formal process began and was so successful that in 1875 Pope Pius IX solemnly declared, "It is safe to proceed with the beatification of Venerable Alonso de Orozco." At the same time, he ordered the publication of an apostolic letter in the form of a brief in which a specific date was set for the solemn beatification in the Vatican Basilica. The event, marked by no little pomp and ceremony, and by great joy and satisfaction on the part of the Augustinian Friars, took place on 15 January of 1882.

Fray Alonso de Orozco never wanted to provide a portrait of himself.
Nevertheless he was painted twice in his lifetime. The first was by deceit.
King Philip II detained Blessed Alonso in his study while outside, from a
window, a painter, Alonso Sánchez Coello, sketched him. Doña Maria de
Aragón asked Blessed Alonso to sit for a portrait, but he refused. Finally
he gave in and Juan Pantoja de la Cruz was the artist. The portrait above is
a copy made by B. Maura from the portraits mentioned above and
resembles very much the ascetic, the thin and drawn face, and the man of
peace and serenity.

Book of the Confessions
of
Fray Alonso de Orozco, Sinner

Divided into three books
for the honor and glory
of the Blessed Trinity

 was born in Oropesa, during the reign of the most Catholic Majesty, Isabella, of glorious memory. My father was Hernando de Orozco and my mother Maria de Mena. They moved to Talavera, five leagues from Oropesa, when I was eight. After I had served in the main church of Talavera for some years, they took me to the main church of Toledo, where I served for three more. When I left Toledo, my father sent me to study in Salamanca, where an older brother of mine was a student; there the Lord bestowed on us the favor of the religious habit, which we both took at the same time in the monastery of our father, Saint Augustine.

Fray Alonso preaching to the King and Queen and the Royal Court.

Prologue to the Confessions

hrist Jesus, my Creator and Savior, it is my desire to imitate in a small way the profound humility of your great servant, my father, Saint Augustine, who wrote thirteen books of *Confessions* for your glory and as an example for Christians, so that they might willingly go to sacramental confession and tell their sins in secret to a representative of your mercy in order to be absolved of them. So powerful can love of you be that this one man even admitted his sins publicly and wrote them down himself, so that not only the people of his own day but those yet to be born might read and know of the gifts and favors which his soul received, as well as the sins he had committed.

Moved by this example, my King and my Glory, I resolved to write these three books of my own "confessions." In them I report the many mercies you have shown me, even before my birth. For you went before me with sweet blessings (Ps 21:4) in order that your goodness might shine out more brilliantly in this sinner. In the course of my life down to this, my eightieth year, your mercy has not ceased to enrich with its gifts a soul that is unworthy of even the least of them. I implore you, Lord, to forgive my ingratitude and the negligence I have shown in your service, despite my being so indebted to you at every moment.

I also write down my sins, in order that after my death, if you so ordain, this document may come into the hands of some of the faithful who will thank and praise you, Lord, for your kind and holy dealings with me and who, seeing my sins, will pray for me that I may forever enjoy the vision of you in heaven. Amen.

Book I

Chapter 1

decided to confess my sin to the Lord against myself; and you, Lord, have forgiven the wickedness of my fault (Ps 32:5). My Lord and God, Creator of all things, it was holy King David who spoke these words, and for my consolation I have applied them to myself for many years now. Being guilty, he uttered them with great sorrow in the presence of your divine majesty; I, who am also a sinner, often repeat them with mouth and heart, even if only in a lukewarm way.

Heavenly King, your mercy is great, and no created mind can grasp it, for the infinite cannot be enclosed in what is inevitably limited and finite. My God and my Glory, your mercy and your being go hand in hand and are coequal; and since your essence is infinite, reason tells us that your mercy and pity are likewise infinite. This explains those sweet and marvelous words of your holy prophet, *If the wicked do penance for their sins which they have committed, and keep all my commandments . . . living they shall live, and shall not die. I will not remember all their iniquities that they have done* (Ez 18:21-22).

O Father of mercies and God of my heart! What great generosity, what unmatched magnanimity! Who is the offender but a little earthworm? And the offended is none other than the Creator of all things, the God whom the angels worship, the supreme Majesty! All powerful Lord, how can you pay heed to a worm like me and forgive my evil deeds if I repent of them, confess them, and humble myself at the feet of your representative, the confessor? Is so great a reward to be mine for such little labor? And, even more wonderful, you assure me that "living I shall live"; that even before the final payment

— glory — is mine, I shall possess here below the new life of grace with its great contentment and peace.

May every creature praise and extol you, King of glory! Just as sinners die a twofold death (Gn 2:17) if they persist in their sin, so in your marvelous mercy you ordain and make it a law that souls converted shall live a twofold life in this present mortal life and when they enjoy you.

Moreover, Lord, you assure me that your forgiveness will be so real and complete that you will not even remember my sins. Blessed be you! Human beings in this life may forgive some hurt done to them, but the hurt usually leaves some trace; they do not forget it for many days afterward, and at times the devil even keeps the memory of the injury alive for years. But that is why they are what they are: weak people of little worth. You, however, my God and my Glory, are what you are: a bottomless ocean of love. Proof of this truth and of your promise is the mercy you showed to Zacchaeus the tax collector (Lk 19:6), at whose table you sat on the day when you forgave him his sins and called him a true child of Abraham. Proof again is the humility with which you shared a meal with Saint Matthew (Mt 9:10) and other tax collectors, despite the disapproval of the Pharisees.

Alerted by such words and made confident by such pledges, I resolved, Lord of my soul, to write down my sins in this book, after having often, by your grace, confessed them in the sacrament. I do so in order that if any read them, they may praise your grace and mercy and also pray for me, a sinner.

Chapter 2

Two Types of Confession

onfess the Lord, for he is good; for his mercy endures for ever (Ps 118:1). There are two types of confession, my Lord, as King David teaches us and as the divine scriptures declare in various places. One type is the confession of praise, given to your divine majesty because you are not only good but goodness itself. Angels and human beings are good, but as it were by reason of an "accident," that is, something that can be present or taken away; it is your favor and holy love that makes them pleasing and good; without it they are hideous monsters because of the hideous abomination of sin. Thus Lucifer, though by nature so splendid when he came from your creative hand, and though an angel by your favor, lost all this by his insane presumption and became a demon (Is 14:2). We must say the same of a human being who is in mortal sin and has lost your friendship and love.

That is why you, my redeemer, told us: *No one is good but God alone* (Mk 10:18). The eternal God alone is good by his essence; he alone possesses goodness from himself. Praise him, for he is good. David urges us to this praise, because God's goodness obliges us to praise him even if he were not to reward us. *Praise the Lord, and do not cease praising him, for he is above all praise* (Sir 43:33). He is so good that when you open your mouth to praise him, you are filled with virtue and strength. Happy the soul that soars so high as almost to forget all riches and blessings, temporal or spiritual; contemplating that ocean of indescribable goodness, it sings praises to its creator and redeemer. Praise the Lord, for he is good and a fountain and wellspring of incomprehensible goodness, in which everything that is good and holy shares.

Therefore, my soul, praise this Lord in whose praise the angels and citizens of heaven are occupied. Praise him for his great mercy that has been since the beginning, for having made this world so beautiful, so orderly and harmonious, and at the same time so useful, and this without diminishing himself. What a clear proof of his great goodness and mercy! A philosopher, guided only by the light of reason, said, "The reason why God made this world was his own goodness" (Plato). The one God is alone and yet has companions in eternity: he is alone because he is one by his essence; he has companions because in this one God there are three persons, the Father, the Son, and the Holy Spirit. He is utterly happy and glorious in himself, but because he is good and merciful and wanted to enrich his creatures by sharing his wealth with them, he decided to create this entire universe. *Bless and glorify your Lord, my soul; everything that is in me, bless his holy name* (Ps 101:1).

O Jesus, salvation of our souls, glory of the angels, grant me light and wisdom. Empower my understanding so that in these confessions I may praise you with my whole heart and my inmost self. I desire to begin by praising your goodness and mercy, counting your gifts as they came to me in the course of my life. Further on, I shall also confess my sins. Help me with your grace! To this end I take as my intercessor your most pure virginal Mother and, along with her, all your friends, the citizens of the heavenly Jerusalem that is our mother.

Chapter 3

The Favors I Received Before My Birth: The Creation of My Soul

rom my mother's womb, O Lord, you are my God (Ps 22:11). In this verse, Lord, the prophet David acknowledges a singular favor which he and all of us have received from your generous and even lavish hand, namely, that initial existence which you gave us by creating us. My Lord, I was nothing; out of sheer goodness you gave me existence, and indeed an outstanding existence that is superior to that of all other visible creatures. For in my soul I am brother to the angels and have been created in your image and likeness so that I may love you with all my heart, since in the nature of things likeness leads to love. You created my soul from nothing, in order that having no kinship with any creature I might love naught but you, O mighty creator.

I give thanks to you, my glory, for this capital, unmerited gift. O my soul — more excellent than the heavens and roomier than they because you are able to receive and possess your creator, who dwells in you through grace in this mortal life and in whom you dwell through glory after this life — what tongue or what words can properly extol so noble a work? Glory be to a Lord who is so mighty and so much a merciful Father, and who has so exalted you! *God is a Spirit* (Jn 4:24), and in order that you might by loving him become one spirit with him, he sent into you an immortal spirit that will never cease to exist. You owe everything to him who created you.

Be not ungrateful, therefore, but say with the bride: *I have found my beloved; I will hold him and not let him go. I will take him to my mother's retreat* (Cant 3:4) within my heart, that I may cling more tightly to him. *I will hold him* with fetters that will bring him not affliction but great contentment. *I will hold him prisoner* with chains of love, which are stronger than steel, with groanings and prayers, tears and sighs, in which he finds delight. *I will not let him go* by causing him any displeasure; I will be watchful and with great circumspection will keep myself free of all sin, while humbly begging his grace to that end. Night and day I will say to him, *My King, grant that from my mother's womb* I may be your creature; I will say, *You are my God* who created me; I am the work of your mighty hands; *be not separated from me,* do not abandon me, my God, *for trouble is near* (Ps 22:11).

The devil with furious envy, the world with its lies and betrayals, and the flesh, ready like another Delilah to seduce the mighty Samson (Jgs 16:19) — all these have banded together and conspired to persecute me and separate me from you, my Lord and my protector. I beg you, sovereign majesty, not to abandon me, for there is no one to help me if you fail me. What service can creatures do me, when they are so natively feeble and insufficient even to themselves? You are my refuge, you are my power and my strength. You, in short, are my creator and Lord, by whose favor I shall have courage to face all my spiritual enemies and say with your Apostle: *I can do all things in the Lord who strengthens me* (Phil 4:13).

Chapter 4

The Praise Due to God
for the Formation of the Body

ou formed me, Lord, and placed your hand upon me (Ps 139:5). Almighty Lord, as of old *you formed the body of our father Adam from a little mud and, breathing into his face, created his soul and infused it into him* (Gn 2:7), so in my mother's womb you formed my body and, when it was formed, you created my soul and infused it into that body. How many favors I received in that one gift and favor! How many people are born disabled and crippled, blind and injured, yet from all these dangers your great goodness delivered me!

I give you endless thanks, and may all of creation thank you for me. Lord, if I ought to thank you for each of my fingers and for each sense, what praise and service do I not owe you for all of them combined! When the blind man whom you healed at Jericho had received his sight he followed you (Lk 18:42-43) and became your disciple in thanksgiving for the one sense restored to him. How much more should one who has received all of them serve and love and praise you constantly? Almighty Lord, let me not grow forgetful of these gifts or show ingratitude — that appalling vice that blocks the flow of your mercies.

You give generously and with open hands, but you also demand a strict account of the use made of the talents you bestow, so that human beings may trade with them and give them back to you with interest. My father, Saint Augustine, is filled with wonder at this and says, "My God, you have need of nothing, and yet do you demand your gifts back with interest?" (*Handbook*). Here, in fact, your goodness shines out more than ever, my Lord, for if you call on me to praise you, it is that I may be the more enriched and my glory may increase.

I think, my King, of the words you said when you healed ten lepers but only one returned to praise and thank you. You spoke with deep feeling and said, *Did I not heal ten? Where, then, are the other nine?* (Lk 17:17-18). Your words are fiery sparks of love that inspire my soul to love you more, Lord of the world. Flaming torches will I call them, that until the world ends will set the hearts of your servants on fire.

You feel our ingratitude deeply because of the great loss it means for us — since you yourself remain no less rich than before. You show us the ugliness of ingratitude, that appalling monstrosity in our world. A dog, which is but a brute animal, acknowledges the food its master gives it and follows him wherever he goes, and even comes to his aid when he is attacked. A lion abates its ferocity and bows down to one who feeds it and pampers it. How much more should human beings, who are rational creatures, be grateful and serve and praise him who created them out of nothing and redeemed them with his own blood and life?

O my Glory, forgive me for my ingratitude in not praising your majesty but behaving worse than an animal that lacks understanding. Nor do the animals alone shame me for my ingratitude; even the very earth cries out against me and reproaches me for my forgetfulness, for it gives back to the sower more than it has received. The tree repays the gardener for his toil and serves him by producing fruit. My God, I too am a tree which your hand has planted in the orchard of your Roman Church. Bless me that I may not prove barren but may yield the fruit of constant service and praise, because that is only just.

Chapter 5

The Blessing of Conservation

ord, *you placed your hand upon me* (Ps 129:5). Not without reason did David add these words in which he declares the great blessing of conservation. What would I have gained by being created, if to that favor you had not added this other, Lord of the world? If you did not place your mighty hand upon me and preserve my being and my life, I would return to the source from which I came, which is nothingness.

You created and infused my soul when my body was organized and ready for it; then you continued to conserve my life. In your mercy you conserve at every hour and moment the being I first received from you. How many times over have I owed you my being and my life! Lord, how many treasures lie hidden in this gift of conservation! How greatly obliged I am to say with the holy prophet, *I will bless the Lord at all times, and his praise shall be ever in my mouth!* (Ps 34:1). In prosperity and adversity, in health and sickness, in sadness and joy I will not cease to do my duty by praising and thanking my God and Lord for creating me and for sustaining me in the being he had once given to me. "The praise of God shall be ever in my mouth."

O sweetest Lord, how weak I am for so lofty a task! Rule my tongue, that it may ever devote itself to so noble a duty and never lose heart. *Put a door there with your holy hand* (Ps 141:3), and be yourself the doorkeeper so that the door may not open except to bless you and to comfort and instruct my neighbors. If you are the guardian of my tongue, it will never get out of control by swearing or cursing or attacking the reputation of another. Sweet Jesus, salvation of my soul, how often I have offended you with my tongue, which you gave me that I might praise and thank you always! Forgive me and grant me virtue that I may never offend you again. It is written that *it is for the Lord to govern the tongue* (Prv 16:1); this authority belongs to you alone. *I place myself in your hands, and I entrust my lot to you* (Ps 31:6.16), O most kind Father and deep ocean of mercy.

And since you so often place your blessed hand upon me and give me being, and since you so often give me life (every time you conserve these gifts!), I pray that in your infinite goodness your holy love would conserve my soul by directing my heart and thoughts to consideration of what I am — a poor, weak beggar — and what you are — the mighty, omnipotent Lord of all creation. May I praise and serve you, my Father and creator, and in loving you to whom I owe everything may I love myself and find my occupation, abandoning all else for love of you, since it is for this that I was created and not to seek my end in the vileness of creatures.

Chapter 6

A Special Favor
Which the Lord Granted to Me
Before My Birth

rom my mother's womb the Lord remembered my name (Is 49:1). It was Isaiah, that famous prophet and great servant of yours, Lord, who spoke these words in acknowledgment of the great favor you did for him by remembering his name even before he was born and when he had not yet done you any service. Every day, and especially during the supreme mystery of the Mass when I hold your most holy body in my hands before communion, I, too, though unworthy, thank you silently in my heart, repeating the words of the great prophet Isaiah, *Hear, O islands, and give heed, you distant peoples, for when I was still in my mother's womb the Lord called me and remembered my name* (Is 49:1).

My Savior, you know very well what my mother told me, for your glory and my great joy, over forty years ago in Talavera, the first time she saw me in religious garb. "Son," she said, "while I was pregnant with you I was wondering to which saint I should dedicate you if you were a boy, or, if you were a girl, which saint I should invoke in your behalf and give you her name." My mother, whose name was Maria and who was very devoted to your own glorious Mother, was your servant, and she did the same thing every time she was pregnant. She told me, further, that "to two of my sons I gave the name of their uncle and their father, Hernando, and the Lord took both of them from me as baptized children. I determined from that time forward never again to give my children names from the family line but only the names of saints."

"One night as I was lying awake and asking our Lord Jesus Christ to let me know which saint's name I should give you at your holy baptism, I heard a very sweet woman's voice saying to me, 'What else are you to call him but Alonso?' I was filled with joy because the most Blesssed Virgin Mary, whose inter-cession I was invoking, had visited me and told me of her precious Son's will. Thus I learned two things: first, that my child would be a male, and, second, that since blessed Saint Ildefonsus was so zealous a defender of the virginal purity of this queen of heaven, she would be pleased if I set you on the road to the ecclesiastical state so that you might become a priest of this mistress of the world. Therefore, as early as the day of your baptism I refused to let you wear clothes em-broidered with silk, but only plain white ones, and I said, 'I have dedicated this child to be a priest of the Mother of God, the Most Holy Virgin, and therefore I want any clothing he wears to be white.' " That is what Maria, my mother and your servant, said, and Hernando, my father, was pleased with this promise.

Sovereign King, how my soul ought to praise you for these favors which I so little deserve. I offer your divine majesty endless thanks for disposing that I should be born of Catholic and Christian parents who rejected the world and the burden-some tribute it exacts, and even before my birth dedicated me to your service. My soul also praises you for remembering my name and declaring it through the mouth of your holy Mother: *And how did I deserve to have the Mother of my Lord and redeemer come to me?* (Lk 1:43). These favors, my glory and my God, were pledges of the great mercies you were to bestow on me in the future. Because you are what you are, Father of mercies, grant me the great favor of never forgetting through-out my life to praise and serve you and to thank your kindly Mother as well. Creator of the world, I am your debtor since before my birth; may my sins not prevent your mercies from increasing in me and becoming ever greater for your glory.

Chapter 7

How Great Is the Mercy
of Our Lord Jesus Christ

reat, O Lord, is your mercy to me (Ps 86:13). In many of the psalms, sweet Lord, the prophet David magnifies and praises your mercy and claims that it fills the earth (Ps 33:5) and the heavens as well and indeed all of creation. For since you are wholly mercy and at the same time infinite, everything you created must necessarily be full of your mercy. Even in hell where the demons and the condemned children of Adam suffer such rigorous punishment at the hands of your divine justice, even there your sweet mercy shines forth, since you do not punish them with the ultimate punishment they deserve as traitors to their creator and Lord: the punishment of annihilation. It is a universal rule that you reward the just more richly than they deserve and punish the wicked less severely than their sins merit. As a result, these two sisters, your justice and your mercy, are never separated.

In the present passage, however, this great king is speaking only of himself: Great, O Lord, is your mercy to me. I, a sinner, may say the same of myself, and with very good reason. In addition to the mercies of which I have spoken there are many others about which I may not be silent. The gifts I have received, sweet Jesus, Savior of the world, are your riches, while my sins and negligences are my own doing. And since, as your angel Saint Raphael says in the scriptures, to reveal your works does honor to your divine majesty (Tb 12:7), it will be right for me to obey this wise advice.

I thank you, then, most loving Savior, because even in ordering that I, a sinner, be born on a certain day and at a certain hour, you wanted to oblige me to praise and extol you more. You willed that I be born on a Thursday, the eve of

Saint Luke the glorious evangelist. It was on a Thursday, Lord, that your wonderful humility shone out so gloriously to pull down the presumptuousness we had inherited from our father Adam. For on that day you knelt down and with your own hands (Jn 13:5) that had fashioned the universe you washed the dusty feet of your beloved apostles.

O matchless love, that bestowed such a gift on a few poor human beings! And, marvel of marvels, you did not refuse this great blessing even to the traitor Judas who the day before had entered upon the way of betrayal by discussing with your persecutors the sale of your precious life. O humility beyond compare, that could allow a few poor human beings to have at their feet the Lord of all things, *at whose name the citizens of heaven and the dwellers upon earth and the inhabitants of the lower world all bend the knee!* (Phil 2:10). My King, how can I, who am *dust and ashes* (Sir 17:31), presume to come to your majesty when you are so cast down, so humbled to the earth, though you are the creator of this same earth? My glory, for the sake of that great humility forgive all my thoughtless arrogance. Implant in me this heavenly virtue, the power that guards all the other virtues.

Lord, let these words of yours echo constantly in my heart: *Learn of me, for I am meek and humble of heart* (Mt 11:29). For when my mother, your servant, bore me on that holy Thursday, it was your divine providence, *apart from which not a fledgling falls into the net* (Mt 10:29), that ordered it so. Blessed be you, my God, and forever praised for this special favor that I have described.

Chapter 8

The Great Mercy of God

 reat, O Lord, is your mercy to me (Ps 86:13). In that deep ocean my soul delights to bathe continuously, in accordance with the words of a holy man, your servant: "Lord, I praise your omnipotence; I extol your wisdom; but even sweeter is your mercy to the wretched." My Glory and my entire good, I am one of those wretched and therefore I shall continue with what I have begun.

On that Holy Thursday not only did you humble yourself so profoundly by washing the feet of your apostles. In addition, when you were at table and had eaten the prefigurative lamb, you consecrated yourself to God by giving your holy body to your apostles under the appearance of bread and your precious blood under the appearance of wine for them to drink. You also ordained them bishops so that they in turn might be able to ordain other priests. In this way a power greater than that of the angels (Is 40:12) would be passed from hand to hand until the end of the world. For you willed to be really present on the sacred altar, ever accompanying and strengthening your spouse, the holy Roman Church.

O holiest of days, day of joy for the angels, day on which the world received so great a mercy! O lofty mystery to which our holy faith alone can soar! For we believe most firmly that we have here him who sits at the Father's right hand and is adored by the seraphim, all the heavenly spirits, and all the saints. What pledge of intimate love is this, my God and Lord of my soul? It would have been enough to give yourself as the price of our redemption, most merciful King, by dying on the cross. You need not have given yourself to us as food! But, when all is said and done, your generosity is so great and your love for us is so unlimited that they will not let you be separated from your spouse; therefore you ascended to heaven without ceasing to be present on earth. O riches of infinite worth! O marvelous gift, that I should hold in my hands him who *with three fingers supports the earth and all of creation* (Is 40:12), and that I should contain within my breast, and my soul should embrace with loving faith, him whom the mighty heavens cannot contain!

What greater praise can I bestow on Thursday, the solemn day on which you took me, Lord, from the obscurity and darkness in which I had been locked for nine months, and drew me out into the wide spaces and joyous light of this world? Blessed be your holy name!

What shall I say of the hour at which I was born? Everything exalts your holy name, my God. After sunset, at the first bell that called men and women to praise your holy Mother my birth began (so my own mother told me), and at the last bell, the third, it was complete. O Queen of heaven, how great your favor to me that I, your unworthy servant, should be born at the blessed moment when Christians prostrate themselves in praise of you! Blessed be you, and may all the nations of the world bless you! Amen.

There was another incident that astounded all the women present at my birth (as I was told by a relative, a nun who had already taken the habit of my father, Saint Augustine), namely, that on being born I opened my eyes and continued for a good while to gaze at the light of the candle. They were all frightened, because children have very weak sight at birth and do not open their eyes for several days. Why this strange occurrence, O *true light who enlightens everyone coming into this world* (Jn 1:2), unless to show that in your great mercy you were granting me this blessing: that my soul would enjoy you forever in heavenly glory? The remembrance of this pledge brought no little joy to my heart every day of my life as I praise your majesty.

Chapter 9

The Excellence of Holy Baptism

ou will wash me, Lord, and I shall be whiter than snow (Ps 51:9). Ever since the sin of Adam, most merciful Father, you have provided medicine to heal your elect and cleanse them of the leprosy we inherit from our first parent. This leprosy is original sin, of which David complained when he said, *In sins my mother conceived me* (Ps 51:7). The original sin was a single sin, yet David spoke of many. The reason is that just as a bush has but a single root and yet it produces many branches, so original sin is one but all other sins proceed from it. From this poisonous root come pride, anger, gluttony, envy, lust, and sloth; in short, from this pestilential source spring all other sins.

O wretched primogeniture which none have been able to renounce save two persons: Christ, our redeemer and true God, and his holy Mother, whom, by a singular privilege, divine grace preserved from this terrible legacy! Such a high dignity had to be hers, since from eternity she was predestined to be the Mother of God and therefore had to be exceptional and greater in stature than all the saints who were sanctified before their birth. This is the favor she acknowledges in her splendid canticle, when she says *He that is mighty has bestowed great favors on me, and holy is his name* (Lk 1:40).

It would have been no small thing had God allowed her to fall into original sin even for a moment, but rather a terrible scourge and very great punishment. *He that is mighty*, that is, the Word, God eternal, bestowed this great favor on her, along with many others, that the demon should never have her under his control or as his servant. At the world's beginning it was said of this mistress of the world that *she will crush your head* (Gn 2:15). Whenever the serpent raises his head and takes possession of our souls, there original sin is found. Consequently, the glorious Virgin, in triumphing over this enemy, trampled upon him and held him down, for she was always loved and found pleasing in the eyes of her creator. All others need forgiveness, for, as the apostle said, *all sinned in Adam* (Rom 5:11).

I praise you, merciful Lord, that you willed to cleanse me of that stain on the day on which I received holy baptism. The friends of God who lived under the law of nature cleansed themselves of this leprosy by their offerings and prayers. Under the written law given to the people of circumcision forgiveness came through the torment inflicted on children on the eighth day. Now, my God, ever since your own baptism in the Jordan (Mt 3:16), the faithful are cleansed by the sweet bath of baptism, and they are whiter than snow because of your blood and your death, which are at work in baptism.

But oh how many children there are that die before birth and do not receive this great blessing! They have no source of help and descend into limbo, never to see your divine essence! Yet *you are just, Lord, and your judgment is right* (Ps 119:137). Here below we see how by law one who is a traitor to his king must lose his inheritance, and his descendants the same, and he must then be executed. But our father Adam committed treason against your divine majesty. It is right, therefore, that the original justice which he possessed as head of the race should be lost to him and his children. What would have become of me, almighty Lord, if I had died before baptism!

May the heavens praise you, and the earth, and all that is in them (Ps 96:12), for so radical a blessing that is the source of many others which you bestowed on me after baptism. *At birth I was a child of wrath* (Eph 2:3), but you accepted me as an adoptive son and an heir to the heavenly kingdom.

Book II

Chapter 1

The Power of God's Hand

he hand of the Lord was with me, and I grew strong (Ez 3:14). Ezekiel spoke these words in praise of the Lord at a moment when he was weary and had been encouraged by a vision of an angel. My God, I too shall say them to you and with very good reason, for even when I was a child your mighty hand never left me defenseless. When I was still very young and had not yet reached the age of reason, I once found a sharp-pointed knife and tried with all my strength to drive it into my breast, and indeed had already forced it through several folds of my clothing. My mother came upon me, my face flushed with the effort I was making in my unwitting attempt to harm myself. She was deeply disturbed and took the knife from me. Lord, what was it that rescued me from that danger if not your merciful hand that did not allow the knife to penetrate any further?

O King of heaven, I adore your mercy and ceaselessly praise your power. It was this power that saved me in my ignorance, for I might have died of such a wound. Even more, in your divine counsel you willed to order events thus so that I might be obliged to serve you all the more for having rescued me from such a dangerous situation. Great are the dangers children meet in their ignorance and lack of experience; some fall into fires, others into wells, and still others, neglected by their mothers or nurses, suffocate in their beds. I praise your majesty for rescuing me from all these perils. The evils which others suffer benefit us, and I must acknowledge that nothing could have delivered me from these difficulties but you who see everything and put your hand to everything, being universal ruler of the world.

Your divine hand was with me and guided me when I, then six years old, and another boy of the same age or a little older agreed that at the moment when the Blessed Sacrament was elevated during Mass we would kneel and promise to enter the ecclesiastical state, and we carried out our plan. O infinite goodness, how greatly I ought to love you for that holy disposition, that gift from your generous hand! I do not know in what state that other boy died, for the vow we made at such a young age was not valid. But since my parents had decided that I should belong to the Church (reward them, O Lord, there in heaven!), I obeyed and from my earliest years grew up in it, being quite content to embrace such a holy state.

At the time when I was serving in the main church of Talavera (I think I was ten years old), I went off to the river one day and there found a young man swimming; I was standing fully clothed on the bank of the river. When the young man emerged, he said to me, "Child, do not be afraid; go further in, for you can." I trusted him and stepped forward. I went in over my head, for the river was deep; the current then swept me away, and to my terror I felt myself drowning. Some women who were washing clothes there shouted to the young man, who had donned only his cloak, to go in and help me. He seized the hem of my loose garment, which was trailing on the water, and rescued me from my plight. Later on at that time another young man went swimming and drowned in the same spot, even though he was warned of what had happened to me.

O divine Mercy, who but you gave me this new lease on life? I offer you limitless thanks for having thus rescued me with your blessed hand. In those moments I tasted something of what people experience at the hour of death, and throughout my life I have never forgotten how, although the young man delayed only for a moment to throw off his cloak and then jumped in and came after me, the delay nonetheless seemed long to me. O Lord, what must the feelings be of one who takes a whole day to die? I drew profit from this thought for the rest of my life.

Chapter 2

God Is Our Guide

 he Lord who is our guide will be with you and will not abandon you (Dt 31:8). When Moses was encouraging Joshua, who was to succeed him in office, he told him, *Fear not, but take heart and be sure that the Lord will be your guide and will not abandon you.* Lord of the angels, you bestowed this same mercy on my soul, for you were my guide, as I have already said, and did not abandon me in so many dangers when I was a child.

Your plan was at work when my parents sent me to Toledo to serve in the choir of the main church, whose archbishop had once been the glorious Saint Ildephonsus, that great defender of your holy Mother's virginal purity. The demon, that blasphemer from hell, was using his servants Pelagius, Priscillian, and Helvidius, who all came from France, to infect our Spain with that error. But this wise and holy prelate wrote a book on the virginal purity of our Lady of the angels and preached with holy zeal against those heretics. So effective was he that he drove them from Spain and repaired the harm they had done.

For this service and the labor this great prelate had undertaken, the mistress of the world came down from heaven, entered that holy church with a great company of angels and virgins, and gave him a chasuble for celebrating Mass. This garment may be seen today in the city of Oviedo, to which it was removed when Spain was laid waste and the Moors entered it. From this the devotees of this merciful Mother of the Lord may see how pleased she is with those who serve and praise her. It would have been enough had she sent an angel with that precious garment. But to honor her priest, Saint Ildephonsus, and to teach the faithful how highly they ought to esteem him, she decided to come down from heaven in her glorified body and soul and give this rich treasure to her faithful servant with her own hand. O Mother of him who created you, how eagerly you honor those who honor you and how fully you repay them for their services, however small! O most humble mistress of the world, what a magnificent pupil the school of Jesus Christ, teacher of humility, produced in you!

In that holy church wherein the Queen of heaven walked I served for some years, until my parents sent me to study in Salamanca and join an older brother who was already a student there. I have no doubt, my redeemer, that in all this you were my guide, even though it took a long time for the good fruit of that day to appear. Blessed be you, Lord, for not abandoning me, even though I was unworthy of such company. But when all is said and done, you are who you are and, like a merciful Father, you enrich your children with spiritual blessings.

Chapter 3

We Must Abandon the World

f you wish to be perfect, go and sell what you possess and give to the poor, and come and follow me (Mt 19:21). Lord, you spoke these words to a rich young man who did not profit by them; rather *he went home sad.* So divine a counsel, so heavenly a philosophy, was not for all but for the few whose love of the heavenly kingdom makes them regard as worthless the honors, riches, and pleasures which worldlings so love and seek. The power of these sovereign words drove Saint Anthony from the world and went with him into solitude. So effectively did they work upon our father Saint Augustine that he regarded his rhetoric and philosophy as nothing and became your disciple, bowing his neck to the sweet yoke of the holy faith. Finally, these words caused the blessed father, Saint Francis, to renounce his paternal inheritance and, scorning the world, to dress in coarse wool. The same words also caused the blessed Saint Dominic and other founders of orders to abandon everything and follow you, the King of kings and redeemer of the world. *Leave everything and follow me, and you shall have treasure in heaven.* To their great profit, they traded the momentary for the abiding, the earthly and transitory for the eternal.

In order that I might take advantage of this divine counsel, you led me, Lord, to Salamanca, where you had a great gift and treasure in store for me. My brother was in contact with the monastery of Saint Augustine, asking them to give him the habit, but he did not tell me of this until he had already been accepted. I for my part was afraid of grieving for our parents, who would have no son left to console them in their old age. When he told me what he had done, I listened willingly. Afterward I reflected a great deal on what he had said, and I called upon the Lord to teach me his will. Then I imagined myself alone in a monastery cell, and so pleased was I with this thought that I said to him, "Brother, let us negotiate for me as well, for I too want to be a religious." The fathers very willingly accepted us and, praised be your name, Lord of my soul, they clothed the both of us in the habit on the eve of the feast of the Holy Spirit in the year 1521, which was, I think, my own twentieth year.

Lord, what words can suffice to praise you for that favor? The other favors granted me have been great, for no gift from your hand is ever small, but this particular favor went much further: you called me and took me from a world that is so dangerous, unsettled, and turbulent, and in which there are so many snares and traps to bring souls down. Praised be you, my redeemer, for coming to teach the faithful about such a life, and blessed be you for giving me so great a desire for so heroic a work.

Chapter 4

The Temptations Endured
by God's Servants

 on, when you come to the service of God, stand in justice and in fear, and prepare yourself for temptation (Sir 2:1). Such is the advice which the Holy Spirit gives, through Ecclesiasticus, to all Christians who by God's grace abandon the world and its vanities and embrace the cross of repentance, thus serving their creator. Son, now that you have broken with the world and escaped from the tyrannical power of Pharaoh, that is, Satan, prepare yourself for the new encounters and struggles which your enemies will mount against you. Be fearful, and do not trust in yourself; and fulfill the law of God, for therein is your justice.

It is to be noted that even in heaven there was a battle (Rv 12:7), and that Lucifer yielded to the great temptation of rising up against his creator, a temptation largely shared, since many other angels separated themselves from God and fell with him (see Is 14:14). Nor did the earthly paradise lack its tempter, that venomous serpent who conquered Eve, with Eve then tempting Adam (Gn 2:1, 6). There is therefore no secure place where human beings, while in this mortal flesh, can live off guard and think that they need not struggle vigorously. What is our present life if not what Job called it — a continual warfare (Jb 7:1) and a testing that lasts all the years of our life? That is why the bridegroom, speaking of his bride the Church and of each of our souls, says: "Like a flower amid thorns is my friend among the daughters" (Sg 2:1). Could the danger besetting our souls during this life in exile be expressed more clearly?

Son, be prepared; do not let the weapons of prayer slip from your hands, for temptation will not be lacking. Take courage and call upon Jesus Christ, and you will not be overcome. It is true that nowadays there are no Neros or other tyrants who persecute the Church, but there is Satan, the prince of this world, and he will be present until the end of time. Driven by the same raging envy with which he oppressed the faithful in those far-off times, he works night and day to disturb the servants of God. The Lord of the universe warned his apostles, and in them warned us, that *if they have persecuted me, they will also persecute you* (Jn 15:20). If the demon should sleep (though he never will), the world will make war on the good; if worldings should grow weary, the flesh with its weaknesses and evil inclinations will not fail to struggle against the spirit, as Paul tells us (Gal 5:15).

How sharp and dangerous are the thorns by which the delicate flower, the fragrant white lily, is surrounded on every side! Kindly Lord, and Father of mercy, how my soul ought to praise you in this regard! How can I describe my struggles and the assaults which that envious adversary, your enemy, launched against me when I had left the world and donned this holy habit? Sometimes he set before me the freedom enjoyed in the world; at other times, the natural love of my parents and sisters; and at still other times, the loneliness and harshness of the religious life I had embraced, as he tried to persuade me that perseverance in so laborious a life was impossible. How often I was on the point of resolving to abandon the holy life I had begun!

But, my Redeemer, amid all these struggles you did not abandon me, and thanks to your great goodness I finished my period of probation — a singular favor which you grant to those who call upon you with faith and love. A good beginning does not ensure a good end; Judas began well and ended badly. If, then, good deeds are your gift (see Augustine, *The Gift of Perseverance*), so also is perseverance in the good life begun a gift from your hand. King Saul made a praiseworthy beginning, for the divine scriptures say that he was like a child of one year when he began to reign (1 Sm 13:1), the point being to bring out his goodness and innocence; and yet at the end this same king slew himself with his sword (1 Sm 31:4).

Almighty Lord, I praise your mercy for my having entered upon this holy state, and I thank you that so many and such varied temptations were not strong enough to make me turn back and abandon the cross which I had taken upon my shoulders for your service and out of love for you. It was not my weak forces that overcame those temptations; it was your grace and power that won the victory.

This is the actual signature of Blessed Alonso de Orozco
(Fray Alonso de Orozco)

Chapter 5

God's Punishment of Those Who Do Not Persevere in the Good Work They Have Begun

emember Lot's wife (Lk 17:32). With great brevity, Lord, you warn all Christians to make progress in the practice of virtue which they have begun. For you set before them the frightening picture of the punishment your justice inflicted on this woman who rebelled against your command, transmitted by an angel (Gn 19:17) who dragged her and her husband and her two daughters from the perilous fire that was consuming Sodom. This miserable woman's sin was that when she was already rescued and safe, she *looked back* and therefore *became a pillar of salt.* Our Father Saint Augustine points out that she became not a rock or a tree but a pillar of salt, so that from her others might get salt for salting their evil thoughts and be prevented by fear of God's justice from translating these thoughts into actions and so being corrupted.

Saint Paul tells us that "only those who struggle perseveringly will be crowned" with the crown of glory (2 Tm 2:5). They struggle in a degenerate way who when winning the victory over the foe lose heart and surrender to the enemy. You, my redeemer, said once to a bishop: *Be faithful unto death, and I will give you a crown of life* (Rv 2:10). You do not give a laurel wreath or palms, as the Romans used to give their victorious generals laurels and palms that had already begun to wither. No, it is *a crown of life,* of truly eternal life that you, the King of glory, give to your friends who struggle courageously and conquer both themselves and their spiritual enemies. But you give it on one condition — they must not cease struggling until life comes to an end and death imposes silence in the campaign of the soul against its persecutors.

My God, you had everyone in mind when you preached the dread example of Lot's wife. But it seems that you were pointing a warning finger at religious in particular, lest, after you had removed them from a dangerous world that is afire with pride, avarice, and the quest of pleasure, they turn back to look again at what they had already scorned for love of you.

I know a man who was a monk in the monastery in which I took the habit; he returned to the world and a few days later was knifed to death in Salamanca. Another who had left went swimming in the river and they pulled him out dead of drowning. Still another, departing in secular garb, stumbled in the doorway in the porter's lodge of the convent and gave himself a blow that cost him his life. What are these punishments, my God, if not threats against those who, when tempted to fickleness by the demon, go back on the resolve with which they began?

In this context I shall cite what Saint Jerome says of a monk named Malchus (in his *Life of Malchus*). This man left his parents, who wanted him to marry, and went to a monastery in order to serve God. After some time spent thus well employed, he received news that his father had died; on this occasion the demon tempted him so that he finally resolved to leave the monastery and go to comfort his mother. His abbot warned him that this was a temptation and that he should reflect on what the Savior says in the gospel: *He who puts his hand to the plow and looks back is not worthy of reigning in heaven* (Lk 9:62). He also reminded the monk of Saint Paul's teaching that *the demon sometimes changes himself into an angel of light* (2 Cor 11:14). Nothing sufficed to hold the monk back.

As he was traveling with a good many other men and women, a large party of Moors appeared and took them all prisoner. The Moor who claimed Malchus as his prize took him home and ordered him to care for some livestock. Since he did his work well, the Moor decided to marry him to a married Christian woman who had been taken prisoner in his company. The man said, "Sir, look, the law I follow does not allow such a marriage." Then the Moor drew his sword and went for him; the holy Doctor tells us that if the woman had not spread her arms in front of Malchus, the Moor would have killed him.

Seeing himself in such a dangerous situation, Malchus agreed that the Christian woman should remain with him. She was so much a servant of God that when she said they could live together only as sister and brother, he was greatly pleased with her. After many days had passed, they decided to flee. To this end they killed two large goats, sewed up the skins and inflated them, and by this means crossed the river.

As they went on their way, they saw two men pursuing them at full speed on camels. To escape, they entered a cave; they did not go very far into it but took refuge in a niche at one side. Their master and a servant came to the entrance of the cave, and the servant came in with sword drawn, shouting and saying, "Traitors, come out here; my lord is summoning you." At this point a lioness emerged and seized him, carrying him much further into the cave, where it had its young. When the servant failed to appear, the master decided to enter the cave, saying as he did so, "What are you doing, you coward? Why do you not bring out these traitors?" The lioness heard the voice and, coming out, seized him as it had his servant. Is it not wonderful how God hears the prayers of his servants and how marvelously he protects them?

The next day, the lioness brought out her cubs and went away. The man and woman commended themselves to God and left the cave; they found the camels tethered; they grazed them and then mounted them and came to a Christian city. The woman remained there, serving God in a religious house; the man returned to the monastery, praising God. How often he had been in danger of death for having left the monastery, although in the end Christ set him free! All religious should reflect on this example and not abandon the habit if they do not want to fall into great dangers.

Chapter 6

The Favors Which the Lord Bestows
During Temptations Endured
for Love of Him

s the sufferings of Christ increase in us, so too do the consolations which he gives us (2 Cor 1:5). My God, if sinners were to taste the favors you bestow on those who do penance and are tempted and harassed by demons and other human beings, they would indeed beg your divine majesty to send them hardships and afflictions. But, since they lack experience of a treasure so much hidden from lovers of this world, they follow their passions at top speed, like people ignorant and blind. The Apostle addresses these persons in order to disabuse them, and he tells them, As the sufferings increase in us that we endure for love of Jesus Christ, so do his consolations increase.

Just think of the troubles the proud endure in order to achieve honors, and how they neither eat nor sleep as they concentrate on this empty business. Or of the hardships and risks the greedy run as they traverse land and sea in search of wealth. Or, finally, of the bad days and nights the vengeful endure in getting back at those who have insulted them. What labors these hardened souls endure, so dumbly and fruitlessly and with such harm to themselves! But let them hear this from those who have gone to hell and there had their eyes opened: We have walked by hard ways, and the way of the Lord we have not known. We have exhausted ourselves walking the way of iniquity and destruction (Wis 5:7).

What a great confession and short sermon, that should be enough to convert all sinners! It is a confession that is, however, profitless to the condemned, because it comes too late when their course is finished and when the end of life has already come and there is no longer a place for repentance. But the same confession is very profitable indeed for those who are offending God and traversing such rough passes — poor weary wretches who experience not a moment of peace.

It is a fact, Lord, as I said earlier, that during the time of my probation I was greatly assailed by various kinds of temptation. At the same time, however — be you praised for it! — I also experienced intense consolations and tasted your sweetness, so that I was able to endure those hardships and even greater ones that you would send me. Not without reason did holy Job speak out and say, *May this be my consolation, Lord, that you have not ceased to torment me with suffering* (Jb 6:10). And King David prayed for the same favor: *Test me, O Lord, and tempt me* (Ps 25:2).

What valiant giants they were who reached such lofty heights that they could not get along without suffering trials in your service and thus experiencing a little of the great trials which you endured, my Savior, when you suffered such a frightful death in order to heal us! I praise you, Lord, that in my prayer I was often able to ask you for what those friends of yours asked, but always while seeking your grace and power so that I might emerge victorious. It is not the role of our weak flesh to ask for hardships and labors, for the flesh is weak and looks rather for delicacies and amusements. Such requests come rather from a spirit inflamed with your divine love, wherein your power and goodness are wonderfully mani-fested.

The Apostle expressed an important truth when he said that *your consolations increase in the measure that the hardships suffered for you increase* (2 Cor 1:5). But we can even say that the consolations are far greater than the sufferings, for while your beloved disciples lost sight of you for forty hours during your blessed passion (Mt 26:50), you consoled them for forty days, speaking and eating with them on various occasions before your glorious ascension (Acts 1:3-4). You took holy

Job's possessions from him, only to restore them twofold; and while his trials lasted three and a half years (according to the calculation of the Greeks), he enjoyed a hundred and forty years of prosperity thereafter, as we read in his book (Jb 42:16). O my Redeemer, who would not desire to suffer for you in this life, when you thus console your servants?

Chapter 7

The Great Consolation
Which Christ Gives to His Followers

am filled with gladness, and my joy abounds exceedingly in my tribulations (2 Cor 7:4). My Lord, the salvation of my soul, these are the words of your chosen vessel (Acts 9:15) who was five times flogged, three times beaten with rods, and once stoned, and who three times suffered shipwreck in your service (2 Cor 11:24-25). Yet despite all these adversities he claims that he was filled with gladness and that his joy was exceedingly great and that he could share it with his neighbors.

Lord, how great are the wonders you work in those who love you, so that they praise you more and more and desire to suffer even more for you! *After being flogged and insulted, the apostles went away rejoicing at being found worthy to suffer reproach for your holy name* (Acts 5:41). And they were right, for it is no small honor to suffer tribulations in the service of so mighty a king, who is King of kings and Lord of lords. Happy the soul that truthfully says, *Far be it from me to boast except in the cross of my redeemer, Jesus Christ!* (Gal 6:14). What does "cross" mean but insults and sufferings? On this royal throne sits our honor and glory, and apart from the cross of the Lord all is delusion, a flower of the grass that quickly perishes and withers.

In order, Lord, to praise your divine providence, I shall tell here of an instance which I saw with my own eyes. My brother, whom I mentioned earlier, took the habit with me. While a novice, he fell ill with an abscess of the foot, which they opened with a lancet. This was followed by such affliction that for over a year he suffered great pain; they often cauterized the spot, and yet, despite all these torments, he did not cease to praise your majesty. All the religious gave thanks to you, my God, as they saw his patience and his resignation to your holy will. He suffered greatly, and his suffering was caused, even more than by his illness, by seeing me make profession without him. Finally, while he was still a novice, you removed him from his suffering and took him to the repose of your heavenly kingdom. I felt his death deeply, for not only had we been called to religious life together, but, since I was the younger, I now felt I had been left alone without him.

My Lord and my glory, forgive me for my negligence in ministering to your servant in his long and painful illness. You took that blessed soul to its repose, and you left this wretched sinner here on earth. You gave him this purgatory for his purification, and how greatly indeed he was refined in the fire of that painful illness! *His soul was pleasing to you, and therefore you hastened to take him from this dangerous life* (Wis 4:14). I ask you, in your mercy, that since you ordained his departure in holiness from this life, you would also give me your grace so that I may succeed in serving you and my soul may never be separated from you. And since it is a great honor to suffer trials and insults for holy love of you, grant me the strength to find my comfort and repose in your cross. Thereon, with my passions crucified and my affections mortified, may I love you alone and find my confidence in you alone; and may the entire course of my life serve and praise you, my creator and redeemer. Since you are my King, whom should I obey but you? Since you are my redeemer, in whom but you should I place all my trust? Oh, that I might already say with the Apostle, *I forget the things that are behind me, and I stretch out my hands to what is before me!* (Phil 3:13). Let the old self, inherited from the earthly Adam, cease to be in me, and let my spirit live, renewed by your divine love.

Chapter 8

The Obligation of Religious
To Serve God

will pay my vows to the Lord in the sight of all his people (Ps 116:14 and 18). Great is the obligation I took upon myself, Lord, when I made and signed those three vows, thereby promising the poverty, chastity, and obedience on which perfection in religious orders is founded. By means of them, as by three tools, religious reach perfect charity. It is this that religious must work to achieve, for they do not profess perfection but rather oblige themselves to strive for it by these holy means. It follows from this that religious do not sin mortally by not being perfect, but that they do sin seriously if they scorn to strive for this perfection. Pythagoras, a philosopher, scorned the title "wise man," and called himself a lover of wisdom. In the same way, religious promise to work for the attainment of perfection in the school of virtue that is religious life (according to Saint Thomas, *Summa theologiae* 2-2, q. 180, a. 2). Saint Dionysius calls religious "servants of God" because by their pure service they strive to approach and unite themselves with perfection (Saint Dionysius, *The Heavenly Hierarchy*, 9).

The first foundation of perfection is voluntary poverty. This was taught by our Lord when he said to the rich young man who already observed the commandments of the law, *If you wish to be perfect, go and sell all that you possess and give to the poor, and come and follow me* (Mt 19:21). Lord, how free you want a heart to be and how detached from earthly things! But do you really mean that we should abandon everything in order to follow you and imitate your life that is so perfect? Did you not bestow dominion over all things on the first human beings, and did you not create this visible world for them?

How, then, can you now say that we will do you a great service if we scorn it all?

Here it must be observed that God did not place these riches in the hands of human beings; rather, as David says, *he set all things under their feet* (Ps 8:7). From this we learn that he did not give these visible goods in order that human beings might love them and enslave their hearts to them, but rather that they might use them as if in passing, setting them beneath their feet, and might place God alone and his commandments above their heads and love these above all else. Accordingly, Saint Luke says that those who professed the Christian religion *sold their possessions and presented the price of them to the apostles, laying it at their feet* (Acts 4:33-34). From this it appears that our redeemer came into the world to establish a republic modeled on the state of innocence which Adam lost for us; in that state, human beings were the masters of all and subordinate not to honors and riches but to God alone. Thus, because the married couple, Ananias and Sapphira, kept secret part of their estate as though they were the owners, both fell dead at the feet of Saint Peter, prince of the Church (Acts 5:1ff.); as a result, great fear rightly came upon all the faithful.

Blessed are the poor in spirit, for theirs is the kingdom of God! (Mt 5:3). The apostles professed this voluntary poverty, as was shown when Saint Peter said, *Behold, Lord, we have abandoned everything and followed you* (Mt 19:27). It is not enough for religious to abandon riches after the manner of Crates the Theban or Diogenes, who scorned these earthly goods in order that they might win the honor and name of wise men. Religious must aim much higher: they must imitate Christ, the sovereign teacher, and follow him in his humility, patience, and charity. As he told the young man: *When you have divided your wealth among the poor, come and follow me.*

The rich who give alms and engage in pious works offer a sacrifice that is acceptable to God, and they will have a great reward. But those who abandon everything for love of Christ perform a greater work, for they offer a holocaust to God, as Saint Gregory says (in his commentary on Ezekiel). In other words, just as under the old law the supreme offering took the form of a holocaust, in which the entire animal was burned on the altar, nothing being left aside (as in the other sacrifices), so too religious who promise and observe poverty offer a holocaust to Christ, the Lord of the world. He asks for this as a most excellent and wonderfully perfect work that smells sweet to the angels and is most acceptable to his majesty, who so loved and prided himself on this virtue of poverty, even though he was Lord of all creation.

Chapter 9

The Virtue of Chastity

he unmarried man is solicitous for the things of God; the married man is divided (1 Cor 7:32-33). Praise be to you, my Lord, who came from the bosom of the eternal Father to teach us to live this angelic life on earth. You were born of a most pure and virginal mother, thereby teaching us how greatly you love the purity of chastity, so that when it was preached to human beings by word and action, they might struggle courageously against nature and live in holy continence.

In this passage, Saint Paul spurs us on to this heroic work and tells us of two fruits which the vow of chastity brings with it. The first is that it enables the soul more quickly to pray and contemplate your goodness, power, and beauty and to renounce for love of you all the delights that make human beings resemble to some extent the brute animals. "I know of nothing," says my father, Saint Augustine, "that so pulls the spirit down as the touch of a woman" (*Soliloquies* 1, 10). Singleness of soul is a great advantage when it comes to forgetting all other delights and devoting oneself most diligently to the sweet contemplation of eternal things, without being wrenched apart by concern for wife, children, and family. There are no better words to extol this state than those of Saint Paul in this passage.

The second value of chastity is no small thing: a wonderful peace and stillness of heart, and a pleasure which the heart finds in you, who are infinite sweetness, and which it can feel but not express, *because it surpasses sense and understanding* (Phil 4:7). A philosopher said that "those who would have delight without admixture of sadness should take refuge in philosophy." I will tell you something far better: Those who desire spiritual delights should take refuge in religion and love and observe Christian continence, removing themselves from the world and its dangerous ties. The same philosopher had this to say: "The pleasures of the soul that contemplates and practices the virtues are keener and stronger than those of the mortal body."

Lord, what an insult and slap in the face these words are for Christians who licentiously follow their evil desires and never come to experience what that unbeliever found in the natural law alone! *'Be ashamed, O Zion!' said the sea* (Is 23:4). Pagans often reproach the faithful for descending to foul pleasures. It was indeed fitting that the ancient fathers should enter the state of matrimony and that your law should order all to marry, for you, the Savior of the world, were to be born of that race. But now we are in a different world; that laborious winter passed away and the joyous springtime came when you, the King of glory, were born into the world. Now the turtledove raises its voice and sings sweetly: *Blessed are the pure of heart, for they shall see God* (Mt 5:8).

These strong conquerors of self are the ones whom you, Lord, told to disqualify themselves by the holy vow of chastity and to cut themselves off from sensual pleasures. Their reward is the kingdom of heaven (Mt 19:12). Therefore, just as poverty is essential for religious life, so too is chastity, which you counseled and so greatly loved (Saint Thomas, *Summa theologiae* 2-2, q. 186, a. 4). O King of glory and my Lord, how greatly my soul is indebted to you here! For never did I think of marrying, but always had as my aim to follow the Church. Moreover — and for this I give you endless thanks — you always kept me from intimacy with a woman. May it please your majesty to continue this favor for me! For although I am eighty years old, no age is secure as long as the flesh is alive. But the struggle against thoughts is usually persistent and dangerous; therefore to whatever extent I have failed to resist quickly and strongly (this is something you know better than I), I accuse myself and am grieved; in your great mercy forgive me.

Chapter 10

Obedience

he Son of God humbled himself in the form of a servant and was obedient unto death on a cross (Phil 2:8). Self-will is immensely strong, and through its bad use ruin entered the world when the first man did his own will and scorned the will of his creator (Gn 3:6). It was fitting, therefore, that you, the Son of the eternal God and God equally with him, should clothe yourself in our humanity and, having become a servant, although you are Lord and creator of the world, should teach the proud children of Adam to obey and submit themselves to the will of others. O wonderful humility, that the Lord and emperor of the angels should become a subject not only of the heavenly Father but also of a blessed maiden, his Mother, and of her protector, Saint Joseph. My God, when you were twelve years old as a human being, although you were so occupied in the temple, you went down from Jerusalem with your holy Mother and blessed Saint Joseph and, coming to Nazareth, *were obedient to them* (Lk 2:51). From this may be gauged the extent to which tyrannical self-will ruled on earth: that so profound a humility as yours was needed in order to banish it.

Dust and ashes, why are you proud? (Sir 10:9). Contemptible worms, puny human beings created from nothing, abase yourselves and descend to your own center, if you wish to be pleasing to the most humble Lord, Jesus Christ, the teacher of humility. When the Apostle wished to explain your obedience, Lord, not without reason did he first speak of your humility, in order that we might know how impossible it is for human beings to be obedient and deny their own will for love of you, unless they are first humble. O my Savior, grant me this favor, that I may always hold you up before my soul as a mirror for its life! With that model before me I will be your servant and learn meekness and humility from you, as you bid me (Mt 11:9).

My initial being, that which I have from myself, is the nothingness from which you took me. And what is nothingness but less than a piece of straw? What is it but blackest darkness? But if nothingness is all I have of myself, then all the natural advantages and other freely given blessings that I have are your gifts, given to me without any merit on my part. Lord, in order that I may rest in you who are the supreme being, bring me with your own hand to knowledge of my non-being. Seat me in the lowest place, as you yourself command (Lk 14:21), so that from there you may raise me up, as you have promised to the humble.

The Sarabaites have won no great praise, because although they lived in community, each monk was free to do whatever he wished (see Saint Thomas, *Summa theologiae* 2-2, q. 186, a. 5 ad 5). How right Samuel was when he told the rebellious King Saul that *Obedience is better than sacrifice* and that those who disobey are like idolators (1 Sm 15:22-23). The idol of the disobedient is their own will, and they serve this idol instead of submitting to the prelate who is over them. "I was captured not with a chain of iron but with the weighty chain of my own will" (Saint Augustine, *Confessions*, Book 9). So spoke a great servant of yours, telling of the suffering inflicted by tyrannous self-will upon those who obey it.

I am most grateful to you, Lord, for governing me through holy obedience. At times I felt it burdensome to accept assignments from your ministers, and was wearied at the long roads before me, but in the end, after struggling with my own will, I bowed to the yoke of obedience; in your infinite goodness you always came to my aid, so that I found new strength where I thought there was none to be had. You know hearts and penetrate to their hidden thoughts; you know that whenever I remember how obedience sent me to this court where I have resided for twenty-six years, I praise your mercy for ordaining it so without my having either merited the assignment or striven to obtain it. Indeed, if things were to be to my liking, I would say with Saint Jerome, "The city is a prison to me, and the desert a paradise." Holy obedience has placed me on this cross. I beg you in your mercy to make use of me in everything I do, think, and say.

Chapter 11

The Friends of God
Must Pass Through Temptations

e passed through fire and water, and you brought us out into rest (Ps 66:12). Since this life is a wilderness and a vale of tears, as David calls it, who can fail to see that it must pass through water and fire for its testing, before receiving refreshment and rest? The Lord led his people through the wilderness, where they suffered hunger, thirst, and affliction before entering the promised land that *flowed with milk and honey* (Ex 3:17). So now, in order that he may bestow heaven on his friends, our Savior first gives them tribulations and wants them to be tempted and tested. To "pass through fire" means to suffer tribulations of soul, and to "pass through water" means to suffer afflictions and hardships in the body, the latter being much less burdensome than the former.

Not without a hidden meaning, Lord, did your law command *that all the vessels of the tabernacle, the vessels of your majesty, should be purified, though in different ways: those of metal were to pass through fire, those of wood through water* (Nm 31:23). O sovereign King, what does this describe but our daily experience? To your strongest friends you give greater afflictions, because they are made as it were of gold or silver; they endure the flames of persecution and give you thanks for it as Job, Tobit, and many others did. The weak, however, such as myself, you pass through lesser tribulations, lest, being vessels of wood, we lose heart and be reduced to ashes. The words which both types speak are those of your prophet: *We have rejoiced for the days in which you, Lord, have humbled us, and for the years in which we have seen evils* (Ps 90:15). Clearly, if a fine instrument is not touched, its music is not heard and enjoyed. But what is any one of your servants, my Savior, but an instrument that has been built and tuned by the hand of the Holy Spirit? And it is built so cunningly that for angels and human beings to enjoy its music your hand must touch it, so that, with holy Job in his affliction, it may speak and say: As the Lord has wished, so has he done; blessed be his name (Jb 1:21).

At this point, mighty King, I must thank you abundantly for passing me through water and fire, by giving me all these kinds of troubles in body and in soul. Not only did you deliver me from danger on the day when I was drowning in the Talavera River, and restore me to health when I was seriously ill at the age of ten. In addition, when I was already a religious and over thirty and was living in our monastery at Medina del Campo, I was given up by the doctors and could barely move my head. I confess, my Lord, that I was almost not aware of death, for I was so weak that I could not even lift my arms. Then I remembered the penetrating argument which a philosopher used to prove the immortality of the soul; for it is certain that the weaker my body grew, the keener and clearer was my understanding. Then I understood some passages of scripture which I had not understood before. In your wisdom you decided to restore my health, and when the eve of the feast of your great Saint Augustine arrived, I experienced a notable improvement and began to recover. Later on, in Granada, I fell seriously ill from a disease to which two religious of my convent succumbed; the same thing happened in Seville and at Tenerife in the Canary Islands.

In your goodness, you willed to deliver me from all these and many other afflictions, you who are our salvation and the life of all living things. You alone know why. Father of mercies, be you blessed and praised for everything; and may the angels praise you on behalf of one who is unworthy of such gifts. Great are the blessings I have received; grant me the grace, Lord, of being grateful to you to whom I owe so much.

Chapter 12

Spiritual Temptations

 od is our helper in tribulations, which have found us exceedingly (Ps 46:2). Just as the noble soul, created in your image and likeness, my God, is far greater than the rough, coarse clod of earth that is the body, so too spiritual temptations are far more dangerous and more sorely felt. Bodily travails are like blows struck against a city wall; they come as it were from without. But temptations of the spirit wound and distress us interiorly and from within, and they greatly trouble us.

O Savior of the world, how could I ever explain the constant war that my soul suffered for almost thirty years? What blasphemies Satan, that father of lies, whispered in my ear! Saint Peter says that *this lion goes about seeking souls and roars to find one he may carry away* (1 Pt 5:8); when he finds it he puts it in his stomach, which is hell. He goes "roundabout," because he never follows a straight path, nor do the wicked who follow him. He roars and does not bite, like a chained dog which you, my redeemer, have overcome and captured by dying on the cross for our redemption; he is a prisoner and can do nothing but roar, unless miserable sinners hand themselves over to him by consenting to him.

What else but a roar of this raging lion was each of the temptations against the holy faith that ceaselessly troubled my soul night and day? He did not allow me to eat a bite without scruples, or to drink a little water when I was thirsty. How often on entering my cell I turned my head, thinking I heard him, but could see nothing. At two moments this troublesome dog hid himself at your command, Lord: when I made my confession before celebrating, and when I was saying Mass at the holy altar. Blessed be your mercy for allowing me rest at those times and for striking truces, as it were, which my soul enjoyed in no small degree; I gave thanks to your majesty that during those holy periods there was no moment at which that infernal hound could bark. But after I had thanked you for this wonderful treasure which I had locked up within my breast, namely, your most holy body and blood, he was there again, showing the same fury with which he had previously persecuted and tormented me.

Devoted and loving Father, who *gives us the bread of tears by weight and measure*, as David says (Ps 80:6), and takes into account the weakness of those such as we, who are but dust, not only do you give the soul power so that it is not overcome, but when it seems good to you, you raise your hand and shut the mouth of the tempter so that he goes away confused and conquered. Hallowed be your name, because in your mercy those barkings have been silent for over twenty years now, and I have felt a peace and serenity which your hand alone could bring about. Blessed be you for thus passing me through such painful fires, so that I might console and admonish those Christian souls whom your divine judgment afflicts with scruples. I would not be able to speak or write about remedies for those afflicted as I was, unless I had experienced what I did.

I recall that a few days before that peace came upon me, I felt that the lion was moving away from me and his barking sounded less angrily in my ear; then my soul rejoiced as I realized he was fleeing as a coward who had been overcome. I praise your holy name for the years when I was being attacked, and I magnify your mercy for sustaining me with your hand for so long a time and keeping me from being overcome. My defender, never abandon me, for you know that I can do nothing without your grace. But if that grace is not lacking, then I will dare say with Saint Paul, *I can do everything in the Lord who strengthens me* (Phil 4:13).

Chapter 13

The Blessing of Redemption

hrist Jesus loved me and handed himself over to death for me (Eph 5:2). Most kind Lord, how surpassing was your love, that you could love even an earthworm such as I. Far more than David, I can say, *I am a worm, and no man; the reproach of men and the outcast of the people* (Ps 22:7). Lord, I do not deserve the noble name of human being, since I did not follow reason when I offended you who are worthy of being praised and adored by all your creatures as their Lord. Let them call me a lowly worm that deserves to be trodden down by all, for I am indeed a lowly worm that creeps upon the earth. Who, then, can fail to be amazed that you, the sovereign majesty, should love so lowly a thing?

When I say "love," what do I mean but that you set your heart upon me — a thought that frightened Job (7:18)? What does loving such a worm mean but that you give it being, create it from nothing, and, in addition to natural being, enrich it with your mercies? Speaking to King Saul, David said, *How is it that you look upon a dead dog such as I am?* (2 Sm 9:8). Lord, how dead my soul was! For, being conceived in original sin I was heir to wrath and in need of your grace. Yet you, merciful Father, looked upon me though I was a worm and a dead dog, and, looking, you gave me life in the holy water of baptism, and there you named me your son and heir to the heavenly kingdom.

O marvelous kingdom, everlasting realm that will never end! The kingdoms of earth are painful places; they daily depress us in countless ways, and in the end the king who reigns today dies tomorrow; from the royal throne he descends to be buried and become food for worms. Those, on the other hand, who serve and love you will reign in heaven amid great peace, joy, and security, being certain that they will never lose the royal crown which you give them. Your word, Lord, will never fail, though earth and all creation fail: *The just shall shine like the sun in the kingdom of their Father* (Mt 13:43).

The thing that most amazes me is that to bestow this lordship you needed only the nine months which you spent, after becoming man, in the narrow and dark womb of the Virgin, where you suffered no little distress. We, the children of Adam, pass through that difficult time like idiots, without understanding what we suffer there. But from the moment when your wise and blessed soul was created and infused into that divinely made and organized little body, it suffered as one fully aware and not as we do. And if you did not wish to pay our debts by that one act, surely it would have been enough for you to be born in a stable at Bethlehem (Luke 2:7) and in the cold, harsh season of midwinter. O heavenly King, how much my soul owes you for the tears you wept not only then as you lay in a manger, but also when, at the tender age of eight days, you shed your blood in an extremely painful way at your circumcision, causing no little torment to yourself and your holy Mother, who was present there.

O hands of gold, worked on the lathe and full of hyacinths! (Cant 5:14), as your spouse the Church described them a thousand years before. The hands of one who is true God, as indicated by the gold, which surpasses all metals in beauty and value. Swift hands, ready to give rewards, even to those who do not deserve them. Hands not empty, but full of precious stones, of hyacinths greatly esteemed, for you give humility, patience, charity, and all the virtues to enrich souls. Other hyacinths of infinite value are your own merits, any one of which was of sufficient value to redeem not only my soul but the entire world.

Finally, when I think that after thirty-three years of so difficult a pilgrimage and after so many prayers, fasts, and labors, you handed yourself over to death in order to give me eternal life, my mind is bewildered and astonished at it all and can only say with the Apostle, *Thanks be to God who has given us victory through Jesus Christ our Lord* (1 Cor 15:57).

Book III

Chapter 1

The Great Sufferings of Christ for Us

n that day, Lord, that was so joyous and festive a one for your blessed flesh, when on Mount Tabor you willed to transfigure yourself in the presence of the three apostles, Saints Peter, John, and James, after calling Moses from Limbo and the great prophet Elijah from the earthly paradise for this splendid celebration, you *spoke of the departure which you were to accomplish in Jerusalem* (Lk 9:31). You spoke with them of your blessed passion, which you willed to endure not in Bethlehem, the little town of your birth, where shepherds and kings adored you (Mt 2:11), or in Nazareth, where your holy Mother conceived you (Lk 1:26), but in the best-known city of the entire kingdom. For in your humility you determined to receive honors as though in secret, but insults and torments in the most public place possible. How differently the proud children of Adam behave!

Thus, my Savior, you linked that day of great rejoicing to another that was to be so sad and painful and dreadful, for, when all is said and done, *out of the abundance of the heart the mouth speaks* (Mt 12:24). So fervent was the love you had for us and the desire, born of that love, to see the work completed, that you found rest and pleasure in speaking of what you so greatly longed to see accomplished. Saint Peter, being ignorant of this wonderful mystery, did not enjoy this conversation but sought to remain on the mountain. But you, who are eternal wisdom and arrange everything with such great mercy, told him in reply to keep all this secret and to continue on the marvelous undertaking that was so suitable as a remedy for the world.

My soul reflects on three great things, in addition to the many others that lie hidden behind these three. First, it contemplates the greatness of the one who suffers; second, the love with which he suffers; and third, the greatness of the torments you suffered in your passion, God of my soul and life of my life. All three deserve immense praise and elicit profound feeling.

Great indeed was the love whereby you embarked on so costly an undertaking for the sake of a few creatures who are of such little value and of which you have no need. You always showed outstanding love to human beings, both in the state of innocence and after the first sin, when they deserved punishment instead of being worthy of reward. Human beings are witnesses to this love, for they were created in your image that they might love you with their whole hearts and find their true likeness in you. This was also a reason why you, Lord, should seek them tirelessly as though they were portraits that had been taken by your mighty hand. That is why you constantly gave them lavish rewards. You placed them in that beautiful garden of pleasures where they lacked nothing for their sustenance; you gave them dominion over the birds, the fish, and the animals (Gn 1:18), and the wisdom to rule everything. What great love, when even the command that they might eat of all the trees save one was a sign of special love! Among us, a mother who greatly loves a child begs it to eat and take care of itself; you, the King of glory, did not forget to give the same gift to those whom you loved tenderly — blessed be you, O Lord!

Finally, after the great betrayal you did not annihilate them or cast them into hell; rather, you allowed them to repent and you forgave them their sins. In addition, you gave them a livery and clothed them in animal skins (Gn 3:21); this was no small token of your love. But in order to overcome our ingratitude — which you could easily have done then, instead of suffering evils at the hands of human beings — you became man and gave even greater proof of your love in this second way. For it is evident that a doctor shows greater friendship to a sick friend if he takes the illness on himself and endures it, instead of simply healing the friend with medicine. O my good Jesus, what superabundant love you showed in becoming sick in order to heal me, in dying that I might live! O fire of love, ever burning! Inflame my heart with the fire of this love so that with all my heart I may love, adore, and serve you alone.

Chapter 2

Who It Is That Suffers for Us?

 he eternal Father did not spare his own Son but delivered him up to death for our sake (Rom 8:32). Here the scriptures declare your high dignity, Lord. There is no better way of praising it than to say with Saint Paul that you are the Son of the eternal Father and God equally with him (Phil 2:6), not an adoptive child as we are, who were strangers before becoming children and enemies before becoming friends.

O infinite Majesty, how you abased yourself in order to raise us up! Such was the remedy needed to heal our ancient pride. You suffered indeed as a man, but because you are a divine person to whom your humanity was united, every suffering had infinite value. When King David went down barefoot from Jerusalem as he fled from his wicked son Absalom, all his knights accompanied him on foot (2 Sm 15:17-18). If the example of earthly kings is so powerful, how much more effective should the example of the King of kings be, who humbled himself to accept so fearful a death as the death of the cross?

Pilate declared your high dignity when he showed you to the people and said to them, *Behold your king* (Jn 19:14). Without understanding what he was saying, he in fact spoke a great truth, for on your thigh, which is your divinity, and also on your clothing, which is your humanity, Saint John read the writing which says, *King of kings and Lord of lords* (Rv 19:16). You yourself told us this, Lord: *By me kings reign and princes rule* (Prv 8:15-16). All of them are representatives of your majesty; you alone are King, who bestow on them their royal power and royal crown, and you take their cramped palaces from them when the time comes.

Wretched are they who claim that Caesar is their king (Jn 16:15) and refuse the submission and obedience they owe to you and your holy law. Such are sinners, who follow Satan, the tyrannical king of the proud, and abandon the forgiving, clement, and merciful King. O my King and my God, forgive them, Lord, for everything in which they fail to obey you and keep your holy law!

Lord, what heart is so stony that it can look upon you as they mock your kingship and not be broken! There the judge shows you to the people, your hands bound, a crown of thorns on your head, carrying a reed for a scepter, clad in an old purple robe, and wounded from head to foot, and he says to them, "Behold, here is your King." What a payment for our pride, our quest of honors, that you should suffer such agonies in this delicate head that is pierced by so harsh a crown of thorns! And when you hold a reed for a scepter, what are you doing but atoning sevenfold for our frivolities and vain thoughts? Your shabby purple robe condemns the excessive finery that Christians wear. Your bound hands signify that you suffer for our licentious use of our hands. Finally, heavenly King, in your flogged and wounded virginal flesh you atone for the pleasures, condemned by your law, in which men and women indulge who are brutish rather than human.

My Savior, may these words ever echo in my ear: Look, my soul, on your King, the Lord of the angels, and recognize the lofty dignity of him who is *Son of God and first-born* (Gal 4:7); see how much he loved you, and what you owe him; praise, obey, and love him with all your heart, because he loved you so greatly and humbled himself so profoundly for your healing. Say with the Spouse, *My beloved to me, and I to him* (Sg 2:16). He came to seek me out in this wilderness and suffered so much to set me free; he took my infirmities upon himself to heal me (Is 53:4) and even gave his life for me so that I might not die eternally. I shall endeavor to apply my desires and powers in his holy service and to scorn all else for holy love of him. Those who follow this path will certainly possess the kingdom of heaven, where they will enjoy the glorious vision of this sovereign and mighty King, who, in order to make kings of his elect, chose to be condemned as a mock king. May he be blessed forever, and may all his angels and saints praise him!

Chapter 3

The Great Torments Suffered by Christ

he sufferings of death surrounded me (Ps 18:5). King David spoke these words when telling of the great persecutions he endured and how long they lasted; but they are words which you, almighty King, have a better right to say than he had. "On all sides I see myself surrounded, and I am afflicted not by ordinary sufferings but sufferings so great that they can be compared to the sufferings of the death agony."

This was true, first of all, because of the sensitivity of your holy flesh, which the operation of the Holy Spirit had formed and ordered. Just as the wine at the wedding in Cana was better than wine produced by nature (Jn 2:10), so your most holy body was more sensitive and more perfectly balanced than any other that has ever existed or ever will exist. For this reason, just as a slight blow in the eye from a piece of clothing is felt far more than a much harder blow on the hand or foot, so any blow to this precious flesh produced great suffering, because the flesh was as sensitive as the pupils of the eyes. The same truth can be seen from this, that a human being begotten solely by a woman would be extremely sensitive to suffering. Therefore, since you, Lord, had no earthly father but only an eternal Father, the omnipotent God, and since the Blessed Virgin, your Mother, a delicate girl of fifteen, conceived and bore you by herself, you were by your nature bound to feel deeply the onslaught of the weather and the torments inflicted on you by your persecutors (see Saint Thomas, *Summa theologiae* 3, q. 46, a. 6).

The second reason is that your sufferings were not alleviated by any consolation, since neither your glorious soul nor the Word to whom this human nature was united gave any relief to the wearied flesh. Proof of this is the agony in the garden, when you sweated blood to the point of moistening the earth, and an angel had to come and strengthen you (Lk 22:43), although you are the Lord and Creator of the angels.

The point is also demonstrated by the complaint you uttered on the cross: *My God, my God, why have you forsaken me?* (Mt 27:46). No martyr ever uttered such words; rather, when under the lash and in the fire, they sang praises to you, their Creator and Redeemer, so that many of their torturers were wonder-struck, abandoned their idols, and were baptized.

In addition, your sufferings were terrible because they were inflicted on sensitive spots: your hands and feet pierced by nails (Ps 22:18), your sensitive head by sharp thorns (Jn 19:2). Praised be you, my redeemer! How much my soul owes to you!

Your suffering was intensified by the great pain of seeing your most holy Mother suffer too, and knowing that the knife of your torments and death was piercing her soul (Lk 2:35) and her virginal body and her sensitive heart.

Finally, my God, you were aware of the offense which the Jewish people offered to your Father when they persecuted you out of envy, as Pilate said (Mt 27:18), who saw the situation clearly. Then, too, heavenly King, you had before you the ingratitude of the human beings for whose relief you were suffering, and you knew how few would profit from your holy death and would follow their own evil inclinations rather than your holy teaching. An even greater source of affliction was the fact that not only unbelievers and heretics but a good many Christians as well would be so ungrateful for this great benefit as to crucify you again in themselves by their vices and sins, as Saint Paul laments (Heb 6:6).

Savior of the world, all these factors which I have listed intensified your sufferings. With very good reason, then, are these called "the sufferings of death" that beset and afflicted you from all sides. Grant us the grace to suffer with you and to join in imitating the humility, patience, and mercy, along with many other virtues, which shone forth in your passion, so that we may see ourselves in them as in a mirror and, looking therein, correct our faults.

Chapter 4

The Compassion We Ought To Have for the Sufferings of Our Redeemer

 am crucified with Jesus Christ (Gal 2:19). On earth, Lord, there are no riches worth desiring, save to ask you in your mercy to grant us some little experience of the great sufferings you endured for us. Nor can the soul offer any prayer that contents you more. That is why the Apostle, acknowledging the great favor he had received from your hand, confesses that his repose and wealth was to share intimately in your suffering and to be crucified with three nails to the same cross as your majesty.

My soul thanks you, Lord, for giving it this holy desire, so that on many a day I asked you for that same favor. And so you ordained that the illness which you gave me at our monastery in Seville — the illness they call "arthritic gout," because the fluid in question passes through all the joints and torments the sick person — should afflict me from my toes to my shoulders, and there was no joint that did not give me great pain. Praise be you, Lord, for accepting the plea I had so often voiced!

When I look at the hands with which I am writing these confessions and see that they are healthy, I cannot but praise you; I went for over forty days unable to use them and had to be fed by another's hand. During those days, King of heaven, I was crucified with you, my hands and feet pierced not by nails of iron but by that tormenting fluid. And although the flesh felt the pain, being weak and not made of stone or metal (Jb 6:12), yet your power strengthened my spirit so that I never ceased to give you thanks. As a result, you twice gave me hands and feet: once when you first formed them, and again when you freed me from that illness and restored them to me.

You said, Lord, *I will wound and I will heal* (Dt 32:39), and that is how you dealt with me.

Eight years later, I wanted to go out to Mexico to help the fathers of my Order who were so fruitfully preaching your holy law to the Indians. I desired, and desire even now, to have the great favor of dying a martyr: a lofty privilege that is not to be acquired without your grace.

I reached the Canary Islands but, because I did not deserve to share in so great an enterprise, you again humbled me with the illness I described a moment ago. How profound are your hidden ways! You cut the thread for me, so that the doctors, lacking confidence that I would live, said that I should by no means continue on and that if I did not embark on the ocean, the illness would not return again. As a result, though still not entirely free of pain, I had to sail back to Spain. I praise you without reserve because for over thirty years now I have felt no trace of that illness.

It is written that *there are no riches greater than good health* (Sir 30:16), but I regard as an even greater blessing from your hand the experience of earthly sufffering which you grant to those who desire it for love of you. There is no experiencing the insults heaped on you without being insulted, or your voluntary poverty without being poor, or your singular suf-ferings without serious illnesses. I say "no experiencing," because it is one thing to think about your afflictions but quite another to experience sufferings that resemble yours in some degree.

Grant me this favor, my God: to be able to say truthfully, as long as I live, that "I am crucified with Jesus Christ, my Savior." May this cross be my repose, my pleasure grove and my comfort, in order that from this strong tower I may conquer the lion, Satan, and flee all that belongs to the world, treading under foot all its honors and empty gifts, and, finally, that having crucified my old self that is heir to Adam, my spirit may have life and the freedom to love you with all its strength and to serve and praise you with tongue and heart.

Chapter 5

Christ's Concern for His Servants

 will instruct you in the way in which you are to go, and I will fix my gaze upon you (Ps 32:8). So true is this, Lord, and so great is your mercy, that once you take charge of someone who desires to serve you, you never let him slip from your hand and constantly do him great favors. These words which David wrote in a psalm in your name express great kindness, and you are constantly saying them to each soul that loves you and entrusts itself to you, who are sovereign power and universal Lord. "I will teach you the way of virtue in which you are to go," so that you may not succumb to any danger. I shall even do more, for "my gaze will never leave you."

My God, these words and promise resemble what you said to your friend Abraham: *Fear not, for I am your protector, and your reward will be exceedingly great* (Gn 15:1). Do not be fainthearted, for I am your defender and will protect you from the demon, the world, and your own flesh, which is hostile to your spirit. Trust in me, putting aside all trust in things visible. *Leave your father's house and your native land* (Gn 12:1), for you will find in me, in far greater measure, what I bid you abandon for my service. I will be not only "your master," but also "your reward," which will consist not in anything created but in myself, who am infinite and an everlasting treasure. *Lord, if you are on my side, who will want to fight against me?* (Jb 17:3). Let him enter the field, I shall not fear him; and if armies of my adversaries rise up against me, I shall not fear them, for you are at my side.

O Wisdom of the eternal Father, be my teacher on this perilous journey on which there are so many highwaymen and snares that cannot be avoided without your grace. Fix upon me those eyes of yours which are so powerful that *when you look upon the earth, you make it tremble* (Ps 104:32); so kindly that when you looked upon Saint Matthew, sunk still in the abyss of his greed, he left everything, and you led him after you (Mt 9:9); so merciful that when you looked at Saint Peter on the night when he denied you, he left Caiaphas' house and wept for his sins (Lk 22:31).

Look upon me, King of glory, and have mercy on me, for I belong to you and am poor. I praise you, my Lord, because you deemed it good to be my teacher on this path which I chose, under your inspiration, when I abandoned parents and native place and entered religious life. It was you who gave the beginning and made me persevere to profession, when I dedicated myself forever to your service. Because you arranged it through my superiors, I advanced to the lofty state of priesthood, at which all the celestial spirits stand in admiration as they see mortal men having the marvelous power of consecrating your most holy body and blood and enclosing in their bosoms that which the world cannot contain. Lord, can anyone with a faith-enlightened heart see his creator and redeemer resting in his hands and not be filled with wonder and inflamed with the fire of love for so generous a Lord? O *manna, possessing within all the sweetness of every food!* (Wis 16:20): sweeter than honey and the honeycomb, of which the spouse says, *I have eaten my honeycomb with my honey* (Sg 5:1). Your glorious humanity is as it were the wax that contains within it the honey of your divinity. Because you, being God, took a human nature and became our brother, our reward, and our food, it has rightly been said, *I have eaten my honeycomb with my honey.* I offer perpetual thanks to your mercy for bestowing so great a dignity upon me.

As another gift from your hand, obedience placed me in the office of preacher, which you yourself, Lord, exercised in order to enlighten souls so that they might enjoy you in heaven. Grant me your help, Lord, so that I may fill so excellent an office for your glory, and grant me a double portion of your spirit, as Elisha requested of his teacher, Elijah

(2 Kgs 2:9). May I myself profit from the doctrine I teach, and may I produce fruit in Christian souls. I shall never forget the time when, as I slept, I saw you on a cross, and you looked at me with such loving eyes that flaming arrows of love seemed to shoot from them. Lord, what sweetness my soul experienced for the short time that that kind, loving gaze lasted! Praised be you for all these favors that you bestowed on this useless servant.

Chapter 6

As One Advances
on the Way of Perfection
One Sees a Greater Distance
Remains To Be Traveled

hen a man has finished, then he begins (Sir 18:6). My God and Lord, the way of perfection is such a wonderful thing that those who seem far advanced and have traveled lengthy stages see and say with greater clarity that they are beginners. Rightly, therefore, is it said that when men and women are perfected in virtue, they will see themselves as just beginning. The reason for this is not simply their humility, which makes them regard all they have done as little in comparison with the great debt they owe to your majesty. A greater reason is that the more pleasing the way of the spirit becomes for them, the more clearly it shows itself to them.

How great are the riches and joys you store up for those who courageously scorn all visible things in order to serve you! Eye has not seen nor ear heard the good things which you, our generous Lord, have prepared for those who love you (Is 64:4). Rightly does that passage say that eye has not seen them and cannot see them, for they have no color, and color is what sight perceives. Nor has ear heard them, for they make no sound but are a music sweeter than can be imagined, and a beauty greater than that of sun, moon, and stars, and all the fine array of roses and flowers. For any visible thing that pleases is only a spark, a participant in the infinite beauty that is God.

It is worth noting what the Apostle adds to the statement of the prophet: the riches which God has prepared for his own have not ascended into the heart (1 Cor 2:9). That which ascends into the heart is of the earth; that which descends is what God in his great goodness reveals. The things belonging to the state of glory can be revealed to a certain extent, so as to be seen by faith as in a mirror, but in the final analysis they are incomprehensible.

Let us look rather at when, and in whom, these ineffable blessings have been prepared. They have been prepared in eternity, for there too it has been decided to whom they are to be given. The just judge will say to his chosen ones, *Come, you blessed, and receive the kingdom which has been prepared for you from the beginning of the world* (Mt 25:34). And they have been prepared in our Savior, through whose merits and death all the predestined will reign in heaven. *I go to prepare a place for you* (Jn 14:2), he said when about to suffer death on a cross. "Lord," says our father [Saint Augustine], "prepare yourself for us and prepare us for you" (*Homilies on the Gospel of John* 58, 3).

Since, then, the goal to which we are traveling is so excellent, and since the blessings of glory are such that they cannot be comprehended, it is not surprising that the way of the virtues, which leads us thither, is also so excellent that those who have advanced further upon it and have labored for many years to attain perfection should say, *Now I begin* (Ps 77:11). Such was the experience of King David when, having seen the goal of the law of God, he said, *See, now I begin. My God and my glory,* for many years now I have, with your help, been using these words daily to encourage my soul, telling it, *See, my soul, today we begin; we have a long road still to travel.*

Sweetest Jesus, who but you, the angel of great counsel, speaks these words to me every morning so that I will arise and go to your holy altar in order there to consecrate and receive the bread of angels, your most holy body, to be for me as the hearth cake (1 Kgs 19:6) which Elijah ate and in the strength of which he walked for forty days, without eating any other food? I am walking in a dangerous wilderness that is not without its ferocious beasts and spiritual serpents. Grant that by your power I may traverse it in its entirety without peril. That which was accomplished back then [in Elijah] by what was in fact no more than ordinary bread has been accomplished in me by this divine bread, the living bread that gives life to the world and is itself eternal life.

Chapter 7

Three Types of Journeyers
Who Travel the Way of the Spirit

hose that hope in the Lord shall renew their strength; they shall take wings like eagles; they shall run and not be wearied, they shall walk and not faint (Ps 41:31). King of heaven, what immense wealth you bestow on those who dwell in your royal house, trusting in you and mistrustful of themselves and all human support! Then they renew their strength, for those who previously had strength to sin now turn about with the help of your grace and strive no longer to win the world's honors but to be the least; they even desire to be regarded as nothing by all and to be insulted for love of you. Those who turned earth and sea upside down to add to their possessions now love poverty of spirit; they distribute their goods to the poor and cling to your cross. Finally, those who used to walk dissolutely, absorbed in vile pleasures, withdraw and are chaste; they abhor their past life and do penance.

Lord, this is your doing; such a change is not possible without your mighty hand. We have an example of the first type of person in Saint Paul (Acts 9:7), of the second in Saint Matthew (Mt 9:9), and of the third in blessed Magdalene (Lk 7:38).

"They shall take wings like eagles," that is, the birds that fly highest of all birds, "and shall run and walk." This passage describes three sorts of servants that you have: beginners, advanced, and perfect. Beginners walk; the advanced run; the perfect fly. It is good to walk in your service; it is better to run; best of all is to fly. It is not surprising that among the four holy animals the eagle is a flier, for it is born with wings; but that the man, the ox, and the lion should also fly, as the prophet says they do (Ez 1:10), that indeed seems marvelous and utterly novel, but for you, Lord, who greatly magnify your friends, it is very easy. These three states are represented in the parable of the wheat that produces three kinds of fruit in the soil of the Church: one thirtyfold, another sixtyfold, and still another a hundredfold (Mk 4:8). Those who walk, the beginners, produce fruit thirtyfold; those who run produce twice that; and those who fly surpass all.

We find an example of all three in David. He says that he used to walk in your commandments (Ps 119:1). In the same psalm he says, *I have run the way of your commandments* (v. 32). But he also flew when lifted up in ecstasy, for he says elsewhere, *I shall never be moved* (Ps 29:7). If your elect do not feel their labors, it is because you so favor them with your grace that it seems to them as though they were being carried by others, as Moses says of your people in his Canticle (Dt 32:11). O mighty eagle, Lord of the world, may you see our weakness and carry us, and receive us upon your wings. What are these wings but the arms you stretched out on the cross when you paid for all the sins of the world? With such strength as this to sustain us, the labor of prayer, fasting, and penance is not felt. And if the love of Rachel, a corruptible creature, so satisfied Jacob that he gave seven years of service in the very laborious occupation of shepherd (Gn 29:18), how much more, my Lord, can holy love of you draw comfort from the labors in which your servants find their delight even during this mortal life?

My God and my hope, I humbly beg you that I may be at least one of the beginners and walk always in the way of your holy law, ever moving forward, that is, not losing heart in so important a matter as the salvation of my soul. I see that I am asking little of you, Lord, since you are almighty; but to me, who deserve nothing, it is a great thing to be the companion of the least in your Church. I therefore invoke the merits of your holy Mother and of all your saints and elect. Lord, in your infinite goodness hear me! And since I knock on the door of your great mercy, do not close it against me.

Chapter 8

How Greatly Human Beings Are Indebted to God for Benefits Received

hat shall I give to the Lord for all the blessings he has given to me? (Ps 116:12). This holy king, David, had a great concern and was much exercised, but not as to how he might win greater honors nor how he might become richer (concerns, these, that deeply affect mortals in the present life). One thought preoccupied him and kept him from sleep, as he said in his heart, "How shall I serve my God so as to please him, and what shall I offer him in repayment for such great blessings as I have received from his generous hand?"

I was a poor shepherd (1 Sm 17:15) and as it were the forgotten one among my brothers; from that occupation I went at my father's command to the army of King Saul; there, unexpectedly, I had the opportunity to do battle with the giant Goliath who was terrorizing the people of God and also had them ashamed, because no one dared go out and challenge him. God gave me a marvelous victory and I acquired thereby a great honor, for the king promised me his daughter Michal in marriage. God raised me to the royal throne and by his favor I won great victories over the Philistines. He delivered me from the persecution of Saul (1 Sm 19:1, 10), who had banished me to the wilderness (2 Sm 15:28), and also from the hand of Absalom (2 Sm 15:14), who was trying to take my life and my kingdom from me. Above all, he forgave me my sins and told me as much through the prophet Nathan (2 Sm 12:13). God gave me his word that he would become man as one of my descendants (Mi 5:2) in order to redeem the world; that was an extraordinary concession.

"Let us see, then: What shall I give, and how shall I serve, a Lord who has thus obliged me to serve and love him? I have one recourse: *I will take the cup of salvation and I will call upon his name* (Ps 116:13). I will borrow in order to repay the great debts I owe; I will present to the heavenly Father the death and labors of his Son, my Savior Jesus Christ, who must come to redeem us; for everything else — my prayer and almsgiving, and even all my penance — is worth nothing except by virtue of the cup which my Savior must drink for me. And although it is true that after I have paid with this rich treasure I remain even more indebted and obliged to the Lord, he is so good that he gives me the wherewithal to pay, and remains content."

Most gracious Lord, I too can say with this prophet, "What shall I give to my Redeemer for all the blessings he has given to me?" Heavenly King, with your own hands you formed this body of mine and created my soul in your image, so that within me I might possess a portrait of my creator and might never forget you but praise you. You were mindful of my name before I was born and told my mother of it, and in the striking way which I have already narrated. In holy baptism you gave me the title of adoptive son; you saved my life when I was drowning in the river; you healed me of so many sicknesses, as I have already told; you drew me out of the perilous world and brought me to this holy religious Order; therein you placed me in the most excellent state of priesthood and even chose me to preach your divine word.

Lord, "what shall I give your majesty in return for so many favors?" I will say with this holy king, *My God, we give to you what you gave to us* (1 Chr 29:14). All we have of our own is poverty and sin. "I will take the cup of my salvation," as I celebrate daily at your holy altar, and in return for so many blessings I will offer you, my redeemer, to your eternal Father, so that he may be repaid by the services which you rendered him for thirty-three years and, at the last, by giving your blood, honor, and life in his service. My Hope, grant me the grace worthily to celebrate this lofty mystery, as I invoke and call upon your most holy name with great faith, hope, and love!

Chapter 9

The Great Mercies
Which God Showed My Soul

 will sing the mercies of God forever (Ps 89:2). My God and my glory, so many and so great are your mercies that no tongue can tell them. From the beginning of the world to its end do you rain down anything but mercies on human beings? *It is thanks to these mercies that we are not consumed and ruined* (Lam 3:22). Lord, your anger passes quickly, like lightning, but your mercy is everlasting. That is why my soul joyously sings of your mercies without ceasing, for you, my King and Savior, never cease to enrich it with your mercy.

The painter who has painted a very perfect picture may go away to another country, but the picture continues to exist without him; even if he dies, it lasts for many years, because he made it out of something and his own contribution was simply the form. You, however, Lord, bestow everything, and therefore no creature can be conserved unless your mercy that gave it being continues to give it existence at every moment and thus conserves it. In you, Lord, we live and move and have our being (Acts 17:25). Great was the mercy shown in producing me, for before I existed I was nothing, and no less in giving me so noble a being that is capable of receiving your glory. But much greater was the mercy you showed me, Lord of my soul, by redeeming me at such a cost to you in blood, honor, and life. This was the great mercy which King David had in mind when he said, *Have mercy on me, O God, according to your great mercy* (Ps 50:3). This blessing was an ocean of mercies: blessed be you for your kindness and goodness!

What shall I say of the merciful love with which you forgave my sins, called me to religious life, made me a minister of your holy altar, entrusted your gospel to me so that I might preach it to the faithful, and delivered me from so many perils of the sea when four times I traversed the very dangerous seas between here and the Canaries to go and visit one of our monasteries on the Island of Tenerife?

But above and beyond all these mercies, O Thou my Hope, there are three which I will not conceal. I always carry them written on my heart so that I may praise you, and I regard them as jewels and pledges which you have given me so that I may trust in your goodness, I who am to sing your mercies forever in heaven.

The first is that during a stay in our monastery in Seville I saw in a dream your most pure Mother, who spoke but a single word to me; the word was: "Write!" So great was the joy my soul experienced that I could not put it into words. Her look was very meek and at the same time serious, and her eyes were cast down; as I write now, I seem to see her still, so deeply did that blessed vision impress itself on my heart. The joy awakened me, and I said, "Queen of the angels, I beg you that if this vision is a truthful one, you will give me a sign that you want me to write." When I went back to sleep that same night, I saw her again, and she said to me, "Write!" I praised you, my Savior, for your very great mercy, and I gave thanks to the Mistress of the world, saying with Saint Elizabeth, *How have I deserved that the mother of my Lord should come to visit and comfort me?* (Lk 1:43).

Immediately I set about writing the book, *Garden of Prayer and Mountain of Contemplation*, and, after that, others in the vernacular: *A Reminder of Holy Love; Rule of Christian Life; Examen of Conscience; Soliloquies on Your Sacred Passion; Victory Over the World; The Art of Loving God; The Queen of Sheba; Book of Christian Letters;* a catechism; *The Lives and Martyrdoms of the Two Saint James; Victory Over Death; The Lives of the Two Saints of Our Order;* and *The Seven Words of Your Blessed Mother,* explained in seven sermons. Finally, in Latin I wrote sermons on all the feasts of this Mistress of the

World, as well as on Advent and Lent, all the Sundays of the year, and the Sanctoral; also *Regalis Institutio,* and an explanation of the Song of Songs. All these I wrote at the bidding of your most holy Mother, whom you, Lord, obeyed when you were twelve years old (Lk 2:42), and whom the angels are happy to obey. I humbly ask your majesty that this teaching may be written down for your glory and the profit of souls who have been redeemed by your precious blood, and also for the honor of your glorious Mother, who, at your bidding, twice told me, "Write!"

The third favor is that when I was in Madrid at this monastery of ours, as I slept one night this Mistress of the world visited me; her face and mouth were joyous, and she said to me, "What do you wish?" I admit that, filled as I was with great delight at seeing her most gladsome face, I did not know what answer to give; when I awakened in a state of great contentment, I said, "Mistress of the world, one thing I have asked, and this I shall seek: to dwell in the house of the Lord forever."

I shall sing these mercies of yours, Lord, during this present laborious life, while asking that in your great mercy I may sing them with the angels in heaven after this life is done. For this favor I take as my intercessor the Queen of the angels, along with all the saints, by whose merits I may acquire this great favor.

Some Special Favors and Mercies Which Our Lord Granted to the Venerable Father Alonso de Orozco As Written Down in His Own Hand and Signed by Him

Some days later, sovereign Lord, you granted me a signal favor. After spending time in the choir by myself and gazing very attentively at a crucifix over the choir desk, that night, heavenly King, you appeared to me in sleep as one crucified, and you looked at me with eyes most loving and piteous. Lord of the world, what sweetness filled my soul at this divine gaze! No words can describe the sweetness I experienced in that brief vision. I remained in great consolation when I awoke, and I said with the prophet David, *Look upon me, my Lord, and have mercy on me!* (Ps 25:16). King of everlasting glory, how my heart remained transfixed by that loving and sorrowful gaze! My soul can never forget that great privilege, as I say constantly to my Creator and Redeemer: "Look upon me and have mercy on me." Let this long exile of eighty-nine years suffice! In your infinite mercy take me from this prison! Especially when the clock strikes each hour of day and night my soul takes pleasure in that short prayer. O Lord of my soul, when from the cross, amid your great affliction, you gaze on one who desires to serve and love you, you bestow sweetness that is beyond description. What contentment and joy, then, will this unworthy servant receive from the rewards which you give in heaven, where you are risen and glorified? This is an important proof and manifestation of the promise you made to those who serve and love you with all their hearts: when this pilgrimage is ended, you will say to them, *Enter, my servant, into the joy of your Lord* (Mt 25:23). I beg you, my Lord, to grant this reward quickly to this sinner. — Fray Alonso de Orozco

☐ ☐ ☐ ☐

My King and my Lord, who can keep from praising you constantly, since you never cease your great kindnesses? I would be ungrateful if I did not say in these *Confessions* what a merciful Father you have been to me, your unworthy servant. During the night of Saint Cyprian, 25 September 1590, when I was living here in Madrid in this College of the Incarnation of our Lord, I took my first sleep, then awoke and began to think about the sermon I would have to preach in this house on the feast of Saint Michael. Then, in sleep, I saw a procession of many people coming along, such as occurs on Rogation Days. Concerned that I would have to preach to these people in this house, I looked at the pulpit and saw that the cloth had been placed on it so that I might go up and preach. As I stood in the pulpit, I heard beautiful music being made by splendid voices singing a wonderful tune and, sleeping contentedly, I said, "This must be the royal choir." The music lasted some time longer than the other music which you gave me the privilege of enjoying, twice only, during that same month, as I have told in praise of you. Awaking I said, "Sovereign Lord, that sweet music was made not by the choir of the earthly king but by your heavenly angels!" I remembered then the song which the angels sang to the shepherds at your glorious birth, my redeemer, when they said, *Glory to God in the highest* (Lk 2:14), and I joyfully gave thanks to your divine majesty, and I shall continue to give them throughout my life, for surely I seem even now to hear that music made by so many sweet voices.

My King and my God, may all creatures praise you in my behalf for so signal a favor. My Lord and my glory, it is told of your great servant, Saint Nicholas of Tolentine, a religious of our Order, that for six months before he died he heard the angels singing. I beg your divine majesty to shorten those six months to six days so that my soul may be delivered from the wearisome prison of this mortal body and enjoy immortal life and the sight of your divine essence, before which those two seraphim sing ceaselessly whom Isaiah saw and heard singing, *Holy, holy, holy is the Lord God of hosts* (Is 6:3). Filled with this desire I will join the great prophet David in saying, *When shall I come and appear before the face of the Lord?* (Ps 42:3). O Delight of my soul, if you are so sweet when *we see you here below through faith and as in a mirror* (1 Cor 13:12), how much sweeter will you be when this veil is pierced and we see clearly? Here below there are no words to explain the sweetness you store up for your friends. — Fray Alonso de Orozco

☐   ☐   ☐   ☐

Mother of God, you twice told me in a dream: "Write!" and in obedience I have written books in Latin and the vernacular. Help me now, therefore, in my old age, to describe the favor which through your intercession I received from the hand of Christ, the heavenly King and our glory. My God, though I am so short-sighted, I shall not fail to tell (because of my short-sightedneess I could not continue writing at this point) and explain something of the signal favor you have bestowed on me this very day, the Tuesday after the magnificent solemnity of your glorious ascension, at five in the morning, the hour at which David says he is mindful of your mercy, which is great enough to delight and give joy to your friends all the days of their lives.

I, a sinner, was engaged in mental prayer and reciting the prayer which our holy Mother Church says on this feast. When I reached the final words: "May we who believe you are in heaven dwell in soul among the things of heaven," I received such a strong spiritual impulse that I repeated the words many times interiorly and said them with new emotion: "May we dwell among the things of heaven." So great was the sweetness I felt that there are no words to express it. Praised be your most holy name, Lord, for because of this sweetness I could for a quarter of an hour do nothing but repeat these sweet words: "May we dwell in soul among the things of heaven"; may we be at rest and take our ease among the riches which God has prepared for those who love and serve him.

I confess — and you, Lord, are my reliable witness — that during the blessed period which I have described more or less adequately, I remembered nothing beneath the heavens and could not have accounted for myself, for I seemed to see plainly your divine majesty seated at the right hand of your eternal Father, and your holy Mother seated at your right hand, as David prophesied when he said, *The queen is at your right hand, clothed in rich garments* (Ps 44:9), that is, enjoying everlasting glory in body and soul.

During that time I seemed to see what the prophet Daniel described: *Thousands of thousands served him, and ten times a hundred thousand thousands stood in his presence* (Dn 7:10). I also remembered what Saint John said in his Apocalypse: that the angels stood around the Lord and, prostrating themselves, adored him, saying, *Salvation to our God, who is seated upon his throne, and to the Lamb* (Rv 7:10); and they went on to say, *Worthy is the Lamb who was slain to receive honor, glory, and divinity, because he was slain* (Rv 5:12). I then remembered the words which the bridegroom says to his bride in the Song: *How beautiful you are, my beloved, in your delights* (Sg 7:6), meaning spiritual delights; for when the soul is so united with its creator and gifted with his spiritual sweetness, it is more beautiful in God's eyes than the sun. There also came to my mind what the same bridegroom, our creator, says: *Do not awaken the beloved until she desires it* (Sg 2:7).

O great mercy of the King of glory that watches over the soul asleep in sweet contemplation so that nothing may awaken it! We see this plainly in the case of blessed Magdalene when she sat at the feet of the redeemer of the world (Lk 10:39), fruitfully occupied in contemplation of his divine words; for when her sister Martha asked that she would help serving at table, the heavenly King defended her. Heavenly King, I really do not understand what it is I am trying to say — you alone understand it — namely, that when I wished at that time to move into contemplation of your precious cross, you held my soul back so that it might rest in contemplation of your most holy ascension.

All that I have been describing did not take place in dreams but during waking hours when I was alert. May you be praised and glorified, my creator, because in your great mercy and not due to any merits of this wretched sinner, you thought it good to visit and console this soul not only in sleep, when it has no use of its five senses, but also when it is awake and watchful. David put it well, and taking the words from his lips I too shall say all my life, *Great is your mercy toward me, O Lord; your mighty hand has set me free* (Ps 86:13). Because of what you are, Lord, that mercy will protect and help me until the final moment of my mortal life. — Fray Alonso de Orozco

□ □ □ □

My God, joy of my soul, I will never cease praising you and telling of the mercies you have shown me, though I am an unworthy sinner. Although I cannot remember how many years ago the incident took place, I recall that while sleeping I found myself on top of a mountain and, looking down, saw as it were a large valley, full of blazing fire; as I gazed, my soul felt a great sweetness that no words could communicate. The fire did not burn as real flames would but simply gave light. And in my dream I understood that your divinity fills the entire world, as you said through the prophet Jeremiah: *I fill heaven and earth* (Jer 23:24), so that by your essence, your presence, and your power you are in all your creatures, conserving and governing them. It is not as though your essence were to be found only within the world; you are not only in the world but outside of it. My Father, Saint Augustine, formulates this aptly: "Lord, you are in all things but not confined by them; you are also outside them, but not exiled from them." It is right, my creator, that you should wish to appear to me in the form of fire while I was asleep, for Moses says in Deuteronomy, *Your God is a consuming fire* (Dt 4:24).

O King of everlasting glory, use your power, I humbly beg you, to set this cold heart of mine on fire; inflame it with your divine love, just as when you came in the form of fire and inflamed your beloved apostles on Zion on the day of Pentecost (Acts 2:3). Sovereign Lord, you know what my soul saw in that intense light; what I know is that the delight my soul felt during that short time cannot be compared to anything created; by your kindness I still feel a great deal of that consolation every day and at every hour and thank you for it constantly.

In one of his *Quodlibeta*, Saint Thomas asks whether Saint Benedict saw your divine essence in the fire which you showed him. His answer is that the saint did not, for he summoned another monk so that he too might see the fire; it follows that he was using his senses, and no one can see the divine essence with the senses. Since this is so, my Creator, I ask you in your mercy for that which I am constantly begging, though I am a sinner: that my soul might be released and depart from the prison of this mortal body, so that it might enjoy that divine life. The saints have no doubt that in the ecstasy which Saint Paul recounts, in which he did not know whether he was in the body or out of it, but saw divine secrets which no human words can express (see 2 Cor 12:3-4), he indeed saw the divine essence in passing and for an instant. It is for this reason, Lord of my soul, that I said you alone know what I saw when I was sleeping and did not have the use of my senses.

During the short span of life that remains to me, Lord, I shall consider it my duty to give thanks to you for these five favors. First of all, that your most holy Mother appeared to me three times when I was asleep, and spoke to me, as I have described. Secondly, that you, the Lord of all creation, visited me in sleep and showed yourself alive on a cross; you looked at me with loving, sorrowful eyes and produced such great sweetness in my soul that tears come to my eyes at the very thought of it. Finally, my God, I will always remember this further great favor, that in a dream I saw the fire from atop a mountain and at the sight my soul was so greatly consoled and indeed is now very confident that in a short time it will, by your mercy, go forth from prison and enjoy you in everlasting glory. — Fray Alonso de Orozco

Concerning a Favor Which God Granted
to a Soul at Prayer

O my God and my Lord, how aptly your prophet David said in one of the psalms, *Who will give me wings like a dove, and I will fly and be at rest?* (Ps 54:7). The wings on which the soul rises above all created things and is carried up to things eternal are its loving desires, which your divine majesty uses; they must come from your hand, for, of ourselves, with our inheritance of original sin, we are incapable of so angelic an exercise, but rather must as earthly human beings think and speak of things earthly. When one has such favors from your divine hand, how apt are the words, "Lord, my soul will fly and find rest!"

King of eternal glory, in your great liberality you willed to give this reward to this sinner this very day, the third after the great solemn celebration of the coming of the Holy Spirit on the apostles and disciples in the upper room on Zion, when I was reflecting on these words of Ecclesiasticus: *My spirit is sweeter than honey, and my inheritance sweeter than honey and the honeycomb* (Sir 24:27). Ever watchful, sovereign Lord, you touched my soul with your power, so that for a while you kept it repeating those wonderful words over and over in its mental prayer. Truly, O heavenly King, the sweetness of your spirit is far superior to all created things, even the honey of which Solomon speaks (Prv 24:13) and which is the finest of all the sweet things of this world. It does not take much honey to satisfy the palate of the eater, who soon tires of it; but the more the soul tastes the sweetness of your spirit, the more it desires to taste it and enjoy its immense satisfaction. Honey fills the stomach, for it is a corporeal thing; but the grace of the Holy Spirit expands the soul, so that the more sweetness it receives, the larger it becomes and the more capable it is of that joy and sweetness. When your majesty says, "My inheritance is sweeter than honey and the honeycomb," the meaning is that in this life souls in love with you taste your spirit who is mingled with this gift as honey is with the wax in the honeycomb; the wax of itself has no taste, but in the honeycomb which is so delicately fashioned by the bee everything together has a savor. What I mean, O my God, is that in this vale of tears, as the prophet David calls it (Ps 84:7), no one, however great a friend of yours, thinks it possible to be without trials and tribulations; but in the blessedness of heaven the soul, now free of the prison of this flesh, will enjoy the most sweet honey of your divine vision; it will enjoy your divinity unveiled. I praise you, creator of the universe, and may all creatures be tongues that give you thanks, because even in this exile you visit my soul with your consolations, though it deserves torments rather than divine favors.

I remembered, while I was in that state of rest, the words of holy David: *Taste and see how sweet the Lord is* (Ps 34:9). How right the words "Taste and see" are! For when the soul tastes your Holy Spirit, it is enlightened with new light and vision; it loses sight of all that is transient and establishes its heart and desire in you, my creator, who are truly infinite and eternal. I also recalled the revelation given to Saint John in his Apocalypse: he saw the heavens open and says that *there was silence for half an hour* (Rv 8:1), thus giving us to understand that in this mortal life these consolations of your Holy Spirit cannot be very usual nor can they last long, because human weakness does not allow it. Here are the words of your great friend, Saint Augustine: "My Lord, you raise me up to a sweetness beyond the ordinary, and were it to grow to its fullness in me, it would be enough to beatify my soul!"

I give you endless thanks, my Lord, that for about half an hour of time my soul enjoyed that repose and sweetness, as it contemplated the coming of your Holy Spirit. While I was in that state, the bell rang for Prime and I awoke as one bewildered and I began to pray orally, praising your great mercies with both tongue and soul. I humbly beg your majesty that you would bring to perfection what you, the Lord, have mercifully begun and that you would set my soul free and render it blessed, along with the angels and the saints in heaven, through the vision of yourself. — Fray Alonso de Orozco

□   □   □   □

Concerning a Visitation Which Our God Made to a Soul in Sleep

With good reason, my God, did the prophet David ask in one of the psalms, *Lord, what is man, that you should be mindful of him, and what is the son of man, that you should visit him?* (Ps 8:5). The "man" was Adam, whom you, the merciful King, remembered and greatly favored. You created him as a most noble creature, able to exercise reason and capable of possessing your divine grace in this life and everlasting glory in heaven. Finally, you created him in your image and likeness (Gn 1:26).

The "son of" this "man" is each of the human beings who descend in a direct line from that earthly father; among them, my Creator, the least, and lacking in any merit, is myself. Why, then, do you visit and console this sinner, not only when he is awake but even in dreams when he is asleep?

During the night of the Wednesday following the wonderful feast of the Holy Spirit, after sleeping for a little while, I awoke shortly after dark and, in keeping with the custom I had observed for many years at this hour, I began to praise Mary, your most blessed Mother. Her name, Maria, has five letters: for the first I said her canticle, the Magnificat (Lk 1:46-55); for the second, the psalm which begins *In my trouble I cried to the Lord* (Ps 119); for the third, the [section of the] psalm that begins *Give bountifully to thy servant* (Ps 118:17ff.); for the fourth, the psalm that begins *When the Lord brought back the captives of Zion* (Ps 126); and for the last letter, the psalm that begins *To you I have lifted up my eyes* (Ps 123). I then said the prayer which our holy Church says on the day of her glorious nativity.

Once I had completed this devotion, I slept again, and in my sleep, Lord of all creation, I heard many sweet voices singing in a manner different from that heard in the royal chapel, and the song they all sang together was the angelic hymn, *Glory to God in the highest* (Lk 2:14). O most loving

Lord, what a gift was thus sent to me from your divine hand! If only they had not so quickly finished that utterly sweet song, during which old age does not cause one to weary and the earthly body seems to weigh not even an ounce! Finally, during it, as the prophet David says, your consolation and solace protects our spirit, surrounding it on all sides so that our spiritual enemies — the world, the devil, and the flesh — have no way of troubling it.

My sovereign King, on other occasions, too, you have in your mercy visited my soul with this kind of music when I was sleeping. For the occasion I have described and for these other occasions I give you many thanks and will continue to thank you throughout my life. I also beg your majesty that, since such visitations make it possible to bear with joy the labors of this mortal life (and that is a favor to be greatly esteemed), my soul, though thus comforted, may keep in mind its own littleness and the greatness of your great mercy and remain more humble, saying with David, *I am a worm and no man, the reproach of men,* and so on (Ps 22:7). And since such great fruit comes from your visitation and consolation, I beg you in your infinite mercy to be mindful of me so that I may be more consoled by your hand in prosperity and in adversity, in health and in sickness, in life and in death.

Lord of the world, whose kindness and mercy shine out in human beings, although you have yonder in heaven so many thousands of heavenly spirits who sing unceasingly of your incomparable attributes, yet you are pleased that Christian souls should praise you. These are the words you said to the soul that loves you, and your spouse, the holy Roman Church, says them back to you every day, *Let your voice sound in my ears, for your voice is sweet* (Sg 2:14).

O love inflamed, O incomparable charity! Though you are omnipotent, yet you find satisfaction in our voices that are so harsh and, of themselves, so arid! But since you sent such sweet music to me in that dream and since you bid me sing your praises, my song will take the form of constantly praising you during this life of pilgrimage, until in your wonderful mercy you release me from this wearisome prison of the body and allow me to praise you in heaven for ever with the angels and glorious saints. — Fray Alonso de Orozco

□   □   □   □

Account of a Dream
Which the Venerable Father Had

Most merciful Lord, I will in a small way imitate holy King David and say with him, *Great is God's mercy toward me* (Ps 34:13). I have made known some of your mercies, my God, in these *Confessions* of mine, to the glory of your majesty; here I shall reveal another which you bestowed on me, unworthy though I am.

When I, Fray Alonso de Orozco, was sleeping during the night before the solemnity of the [Three] Kings in this year, I saw myself descending in a dream from a high place to the ground. I say "descending" through the air, not "falling," for when persons dream they are falling from a tower, they are naturally afraid and fearful because they are in danger of being killed; but when I dreamed that I was coming down from that height, I was not afraid or anxious; that is why I said "descending" and not "falling." When I reached the ground I stayed on my feet without feeling any bump or hurt. As I began to walk, I awoke.

I then praised your majesty when I realized that in the dream I had descended such a great distance without a stairway and that my reaching the ground brought no hurt. Reflecting on this dream I began to say: My Lord, has this occurred so that I might understand the change I have undergone in passing from the lofty state of the contemplative life that I led many years ago when I had no responsibilities, to the life which I am now compelled to live in this house of Our Lady of the Incarnation, where I presently am and where I take care of the sick and hand out temporal necessities?

You know, my Lord, the great difficulty I had when living in our monastery of Saint Philip, for I could not sleep due to the noise made by bells and clocks day and night. Therefore the Lady, Dona María of Aragón, took pity on my fatigue and did me the signal favor of bringing me to this house of hers where I have no choice but to imitate the life of Martha, who was continually troubled as she served the Lord and his apostles at table. Here they also live the life of Magdalene to the glory of your majesty, for in this house the divine Office is said before the Blessed Sacrament, and there are Masses, communions and confessions of the faithful, and sermons. As a result, my King, I have come down from the high place where I had time to live the lofty life of contemplation for which you created us, since I was free of any responsibility for temporal things; here, by your favor, my God, I live the life both of Mary Magdalene and of Martha, for your majesty, from whose hand every good thing comes (Jas 1:17), has given me the spirit needed to exercise, for your glory, the two lives which a perfect Christian embraces. Lord, preserve and increase everything for your holy service and glory. Amen. — Fray Alonso de Orozco

□   □   □   □

Concerning Angelic Music
Which the Reverend Father Heard

Sovereign King of glory, my Lord Jesus Christ, why should I hide the mercies which you have bestowed on this unworthy servant, as your mighty and generous hand ceaselessly multiplies favors for me who am dust and ashes?

In this year 1590, on 9 September, a day after the nativity of our most pure Lady and your Mother, I was residing here in Madrid in this house and college that bears the name of Our Lady of the Incarnation. During the night, as I slept, you, my God, showed me a signal mercy: I heard music in which two voices sang, one higher than the other. I listened with great pleasure; I rested my head on my left hand and began to weep, not tears of sadness but tears of wonderful devotion and joy. So great was the sweetness my soul experienced in that dream that no piping of flageolet and no music of the royal choir can be compared with it. Throughout it all I had no use of any of my senses.

O my Savior, the Joy of my soul, how can you be mindful of this worm and bestow such great gifts upon him? At that moment, to use the words of Isaiah (6:23), I heard two seraphim singing as they stood beneath a very high throne and answered each other as though in choir, each saying, "Holy, holy, holy is the Lord of battles; the earth is full of his glory." As each praised the mystery of the Most Holy Trinity and the unity of the esssence, saying "Holy is the Father, holy the Son, and holy the Holy Spirit, one single Lord," the other remained silent; the two voices ceaselessly sang thus together, making a sweet harmony.

So great and effective was the power this music of a few angels had upon my soul that when I woke I said with the prophet David, and I still say every day and at every hour, *Lord, my song will always be of you; I have become a wonder and a sign to many, and you are my strong helper* (Ps 71:6-7). And in another psalm the same prophet says, *I will sing to the Lord, who has given me good things, and I will praise his most high name* (Ps 13:7).

What tongue can tell the mercies I have received from you, my Lord, who created me in your image and likeness and were mindful of my name before I was born, who called me to this holy religious Order of my father, Saint Augustine, and chose me as a minister of your holy altar, and who, finally, willed that I preach your divine word? Therefore, heavenly King, I will always sing of your mercies, in prosperity and in adversity, in health and in sickness, in life and in death.

O Lord of the world, whose great kindness and mercy shine out in human beings, although you have yonder in heaven so many thousands of heavenly spirits who praise you unceasingly, yet you are pleased that Christian souls should praise you. These are the words, Lord, which you said and say daily to your Spouse, the holy Roman Church and to every soul that loves you: *Let your voice sound in my ears, for your voice is sweet* (Sg 2:14).

O love inflamed, O incomparable charity! Though you are omnipotent, yet you find satisfaction in our voices that are so harsh and, of themselves, so arid! But since you sent such sweet music to me in that dream and since you bid me sing your praises, my song will take the form of constantly praising you during this life of pilgrimage, until in your wonderful mercy you release me from this wearisome prison of the body and allow me to praise you in heaven forever with the angels and glorious saints. — Fray Alonso de Orozco

Notes on Some Passages of the *Confessions* of the Servant of God, Fray Alonso de Orozco by Father Master Fray Basilio Ponce de León Professor of Durandus Studies in the University of Salamanca

I have read the books of the *Confessions* of the great servant of God, our father and brother, Fray Alonso de Orozco, and I hope that they will never leave my possession and still less my memory, so that they may continually have upon my will the effect which they have when read even in passing and in the midst of other unavoidable occupations. "Such is the power of prayer mingled with tears," as Saint Gregory of Nyssa said of the writings of that great Father, Saint Ephrem. Such was the fire of love, such the tears and devotion, with which our servant of God wrote his *Confessions* that it is not surprising their reading should produce effects like those of fire and water.

I learned from them what I could not learn from the author himself, simply because I never spoke to him or saw him. For, fifteen days after I received this holy habit at Salamanca, this outstanding man, who was in Madrid at the time, departed this life for eternal life.

He had a very keen and ready mind, one that seemed formed by God for instructing others in morals. Anyone who reads his works will see this, and the light and devotion one experiences in them will be the clearest proof that he wrote them at the Virgin's bidding. So great is their power to teach, move, and enrich that that preacher who reads them will be able in turn to teach, move, and enrich others. The many books he wrote in Latin and the vernacular, the finished character of everything in them, and the fact that they were written amid so many other occupations (preaching, confessions, helping to heal and console souls) — all these are evidence that the books were written by order of God, who in his work need not respect the delays imposed by time.

The author of the Life of Saint Bernard says, "He emerges far more clearly from his own books and makes himself known best in his own writings, in which he seems to have drawn his own portrait and provided a kind of mirror reflecting his own face, so that what was said of Ambrose seems legitimately applicable here: 'In the praises he bestows he gives expression to himself; laureled as he is with the Spirit, let him be crowned with his own writings' " (Book 3, chapter 7). This passage seems as if intended for my use, along with everything that follows it. I leave the rest aside, however, for I am not writing a eulogy of this holy man, but simply an introduction to some short notes. He manifests himself splendidly in his books; his writings make him known to our profit, for in them he has left a portrait of himself and a mirror in which his spirit may be known — his love of God and neighbor, his prayerfulness, his devotion and virtues — so that his own pen is the best crier and chronicler of this holy man. Since he is now enjoying his reward in heaven, his books serve as crowns.

He was an excellently trained and grounded theologian; the skill, brevity, and clarity he displays in dealing with sensitive subjects make that very clear. So familiar was he with the scriptures and with the writings of the saints that when I read these books of his, and others, I recall what I read in the saints. As a result, I expected to read these *Confessions* without much difficulty and to find in them the arguments and citations from the saints that I found in his other books. The same one performed these wonders in this great Father who performed them in the saints, and so the Father and the saints are very much alike not only in spirit but even in their words.

On the other hand, the spirit that transports him writes with a brevity that does not allow him time to dwell on certain points or to expand the argument and make his views clearer. It has therefore seemed good to me to add to what he says in some places; my words will differ from his as snow from fire or coarse woolen cloth from brocade, but they will help clarify the meaning. My desire is a good one; my work, in my own view, is not necessary if something can be called "not necessary" when he who asks it has power to command.

□   □   □   □

Book I, chapter 1, page 38: "No created mind can grasp it, for the infinite cannot be enclosed in what is inevitably limited and finite." The meaning is: no created mind can grasp it so as to know it infinitely and as the infinite demands to be known. This is the explanation of Saint Thomas.[1]

In the same chapter, page 39: "Souls converted shall live a twofold life in this present mortal life and when they enjoy you." The holy man speaks first of this mortal life: here the just live a twofold life by reason of faith and of grace, just as those who lack faith die a twofold death; "trees twice dead," Saint Jude calls them (v. 12). The writer speaks also of the other life: the explanation is clear, for the just live the life of grace and the life of glory of body and soul, as Ezekiel says, *He shall surely live* (Ez 18:9). But he may be following the idiom of sacred scripture and using "twofold life" to express the excellence of that life; thus Isaiah says, *She has received twofold from the Lord* (40:2), and Jeremiah, *With a double destruction destroy them* (17:18).

Chapter 2, page 40: "It is your favor and holy love that makes them pleasing," for that favor and love are the cause of the grace whereby the just are pleasing to God, according to the teaching of the sacred Council of Trent.[2]

In the same chapter, page 41: "The one God is alone." The theologians agree fully according to faith and speak of God as "alone" but not solitary, by reason of the trinity of persons and the unity of essence.

Chapter 3, page 42: "Brother to the angels" in degree of understanding. Therefore our father Saint Augustine said: "Just as we must confess that the human soul is not what God is, so we must assume that nothing of all he created is closer to him."[3] And further on in the same chapter: "Among the other things which God created, some are less than the [human] soul, some its equal: less, as for example the soul of the beast; equal, as for example the angels; but nothing is superior."[4] Admirable words for letting the soul understand its dignity and esteem itself as equal to the angels, while acknowledging no other as superior save God, as Saint Augustine teaches.

In the same chapter, page 42: "In whom [your creator] you will dwell through glory after this life." This is in keeping with what Christ our Lord said to the faithful servant, *Enter into the joy of your Lord* (Mt 25:23). Joy does not enter into you, but you into joy, thus showing the incomprehensible greatness of this joy, as Cardinal Cajetan said when explaining these words of Christ, "So great is the joy in God to be found in the heavenly fatherland that it cannot be pent up in a human being; therefore human beings enter into this incomprehensible joy rather than it into them as though it could be contained in them."

Chapter 6, page 49: "What else are you to call him but Alonso?" The saint refers to the same favor at the end of his sermon on the first words of the Virgin. Here he calls himself her debtor before he was even born. In like manner, the names of Christ and Saint John the Baptist and Our Lady were revealed to their parents before they were born. This was a singular favor which the Lord willed to bestow on this holy man; it has not often been given to others whom the Lord chose.

Chapter 7, page 51: "You did not refuse this great blessing even to the traitor Judas." He is saying that Christ gave communion to Judas; this is the view of Saint Augustine[5] and Saint Cyprian and Origen, whom the theologians commonly follow.

Chapter 8, page 52: "You also ordained them bishops." The holy man is following a quite probable opinion that the apostles were consecrated bishops on the night of the Last

Supper when Christ our Lord said, *Do this in memory of me* (1 Cor 11:24). The opinion is considered very probable by Father Alfonso Salmeron,[6] and is followed by Father Enriquez.[7]

Book II, chapter 1, page 57: "For the vow we made at such a young age was not valid," either because the holy man thought they did not have sufficient use of reason at that time, or, if they did, the vow was not hard and fast because their parents could annul it. Both opinions represent the common views of the doctors.

Chapter 2, page 58: "Pelagius, Priscillian, and Hevidius, who came from France." Although Priscillian was Spanish by birth, the poison he spread came from France, where he learned his vicious teaching against the purity of the Virgin, as well as other follies.

Chapter 8, page 73: "They do sin seriously if they scorn to strive for this perfection." This is the teaching of Saint Thomas;[8] "scorning" means doing little to make amends and paying no heed to the works by which one advances toward perfection in keeping with the special obligation religious have of striving for it. This scorn is seriously sinful, as Gregory of Valencia makes clear.[9]

Chapter 13, page 86: "The nine months which you spent, after becoming man, in the narrow and dark womb of the Virgin, where you suffered no little distress." It cannot be denied that Christ our Lord endured a hardship in being thus confined, as one with complete possession of mind, in the pure womb of the Virgin, as this holy man says. Were this not the case, Saint Augustine would not say in his hymn *Te Deum*: "You did not shrink from the Virgin's womb,"[10] that is, in order to redeem humankind Christ did not hesitate to be confined in this narrow, dark lodging; nor would Saint Peter Chrysologus say, when reflecting on this point, and desirous of bringing home the weighty obligations of human beings, "It was through this narrow space that God sought you out."[11]

We may piously believe that Christ's great love took account of this hardship so that he might begin to suffer for human beings even before he was born. There in the womb, Saint Augustine says, he exercised patience as he waited out the intentions and delays of nature: "How great the patience of the Savior, that he who made his own limbs should wait to be born!"[12] He also showed it in putting off his entrance into the world and his redemption of humankind, as Abbot Guerric says in this admirable passage, "Of all the human infirmities or limitations which God in his condescension endured for us, I regard as first in time and almost unsurpassed in humility the fact that the uncircumscribed divine majesty endured to be conceived in the womb and to be confined there for nine months. For in what other circumstance did he so empty himself or when did he seem to depart so completely from himself? For so long a time divine wisdom said nothing and divine power did not nothing that was manifest; by no visible sign did the hidden and confined majesty betray its presence. Not thus did he act on the cross," and so on.[13] According to this important writer, the failure (as judged by human beings) of Christ our Lord to work the redemption of the human race through the proofs which his love required of him; his delaying for those nine months; his confinement in the womb of the Virgin during which he did not do what his ardent desire bade him do — all these were among the greatest hardships Christ endured in this life.

Denis the Carthusian adopted the same thought and words in his commentary on the hymn *Te Deum laudamus*; I say nothing of other moderns who have said the same thing. It may also be thought that the Church had this in mind when it deliberately put the following words into the calendar for the day of Christ's birth: "Nine months having passed since his conception"; for if the words do not refer to this mystery, they would seem to be superfluous.

Book III, Chapter 3, page 93: "The same truth can be seen from this, that a human being begotten solely by a woman would be extremely sensitive to suffering." The holy man shows keen insight here as he reflects on the sensitivity of the body of Christ our Lord, for children resemble their mother more than their father in their condition, tendencies, and frailty. "Pueri, ut in plurimum, matrizare solent," says a jurist; or, as we would put it, children are ordinarily like their mothers. This is the teaching of Galen and Avicenna.[14] When the mother suckles her child, she continues the process that began when the child was in her womb and was being fed with the same food, but then in the form of blood. As a result, the defects of the child shame the mother more than the father, as the wise man says, *The child that is left to its own will brings shame on its mother* (Prv 29:15). It is in keeping, therefore, with sound philosophy to say that a child engendered, bred, and nourished exclusively from its mother's blood would afterward have a more sensitive constitution.

In the same chapter (page 93): "Your sufferings were not alleviated by any consolation." For, although there were motives which, if reflected on by Christ, could have given him consolation, he set aside reflection on these things for certain periods of time, in order that his suffering and affliction might be keener; he gave free rein to senses and soul so that they might feel painful things as these demand to be felt, and he imposed barriers lest during those periods any consolation flow over into the soul from the understanding, which saw God clearly. This is the teaching of Saint Thomas[15] and is common among the theologians; it is taught by Cano,[16] Valencia,[17] and others. Similarly, although an angel came down to strengthen Christ, this was to bring home to him his own value and not so console him; these are different functions, as Suárez[18] and Gabriel Vázquez[19] teach in accord with the teaching of the saints.

Chapter 8, page 106: "Everything — my prayer and alms-giving, and even all my penance — is worth nothing." That is, they are worth nothing insofar as they originate in the person who does them; their value is due to the grace that gives rise to them and was merited for us by Christ our Lord in his passion, according to the teaching of the sacred Council of Trent.[20]

Chapter 9, page 108: "I beg you that if this vision is a truthful one you will give me a sign that you want me to write." This was a holy request and one in accord with reason; it was not a rash petition but one that sprang from the humble idea which the holy man had of himself. A parallel: Abraham's faithful servant was not blamed but praised when he asked God for a sign whereby he might know the girl he was to choose as Isaac's wife (Gn 24:14). The repetition of Alonso's dream confirmed the original dream and was quite a good sign of its truth, as we can see from what happened to Peter: *This was done thrice* (Acts 10:16), and from Pharaoh's dream: *It is a token of the certainty* (Gn 41:32).

In the present chapter and in the other sections that follow, down to the end of the *Confessions*, this holy man reports special favors and rewards which he received from God: heavenly music which he heard several times, appearances of Christ and the Virgin which were granted to him, and visions of things most high. Some of these were granted while he was alert and awake: for example, the favors on Ascension Day and on the third day after the feast of the Holy Spirit; others were granted while he slept, and since not a few of them took place in dreams, it is right that we realize these were not natural dreams, like those which people ordinarily have, but transcended the natural order, like those of Joseph (Gn 37:7), the Virgin's husband (Mt 1:20; 2:13), Saint Peter (Acts 10:11), and Adam at the time when Eve was being formed (Gn 2:21), and so too, usually, those of the saints, whose dreams were nothing less than prophecies and mysteries.

Thus God reveals secrets to some of his servants during their waking hours by speaking to them interiorly or exteriorly, while to others he reveals them by means of representations or images which he sets before their interior or exterior senses. Likewise, in the one or the other way (either speaking to them or setting images before them), he is wont to reveal mysteries to his servants in dreams. He spoke to the spouse of the Virgin; to Joseph of old and to Saint Peter he showed himself in images. There can thus be a type of prophecy that occurs in dreams; it is not on that account imperfect but on the contrary may be very perfect, whether it take the form of a locution or a vision. For in dreams as in waking there can be intellectual visions and other visions of a less perfect kind, as we see from Saint Thomas: "It would seem to be a higher degree of prophecy when a prophet, be he awake or asleep, hears words that express an intelligible truth."[21] He repeats the same thought in article 4 when speaking of the prophetic gift given to Moses. In this regard, then, he speaks of dreams and ecstasies in the same way as does Saint Augustine.[22]

The difference between these dreams and others that are natural and ordinary is very clear to the soul on which God bestows them, due to the certainty they leave behind them regarding both the dreams themselves and that which is being communicated through them. For God, who is the author of the dream, is also the source of this very sure certainty and certain security. Such is the teaching of two holy doctors of the Church.

The first is Saint Augustine. Speaking of the things which God revealed in dreams to his holy mother Monica (who greatly desired her son to marry and commended this intention to God, asking him to let her know by a vision whether it was his will that the young man should marry), he says, "At my request and by her own desire she daily beseeched you with heartfelt prayers to send her some revelation in a vision about my future marriage, but this you would not do. She had some vague and fanciful dreams which were the result of her preoccupation with these thoughts, and when she told me about them, she treated them as of no importance and did not speak with the assurance that she always had when you sent her visions. She always said that by some sense, which she could not describe in words, she was able to distinguish between your revelations and her own natural dreams."[23] God revealed nothing to her; and although she had some dreams about her son's marriage, she set no store by them, since they were the result of her daytime preoccupation rather than of any divine revelation. She reported them to Augustine, her son, without placing any reliance on them, for, she said, her soul was able, in some secret way which she could not put into words, to distinguish between dreams in which God spoke to her and others which were the ordinary product of nature.

Saint Gregory says the same thing in words which I shall simply cite here: "Since dreams display so many different characteristics, we ought to be all the more reluctant to trust them, the more difficult it is to decide what impulse gives rise to them. Holy men and women, on the other hand, distinguish by a certain interior savor between deceits and proper revelations, whether these take the form of voices heard in visions or of images. As a result, they know what they are receiving from the good Spirit and what they are being subjected to by the deceiver."[24] Cardinal Torquemada, in his Preface to the *Revelations* of Saint Brigid, cites some other words of Saint Gregory, but without giving the source: "When God speaks directly to the soul, only the capacity for internal inspiration is activated within us, for God's power is known by an indescribable interior and very sweet lightening of the spirit."[25] From these sources Saint Thomas derived the same doctrine and taught it to us in turn.[26] Alonso was favored by God in dreams, sometimes with locutions, sometimes with spiritual visions, sometimes with intellectual visions, as can be seen from the accounts he gives and as I shall note in particular below.

For these reasons, in addition to others that might be cited, I have no doubt that this holy man possessed the spirit of prophecy, and this not just of an ordinary kind but of an excellent and perfect kind. For a prophet is one to whom things future or past or present are revealed which are not attainable by the natural powers of the mind, as Saint John Chrysostom[27] and many other saints and doctors teach. The fact that many of these mysteries were revealed to the holy man in dreams is not a true difficulty, since prophecy in dreams has a long lineage, as can be seen from Numbers 13:3, Jeremiah 13, and Acts 1.

It must be noted, however, that a man is not a prophet simply for having a mysterious dream sent to him by God; he must also understand the mystery. Thus Nebuchadnezzar and Pharaoh had mysterious dreams but did not understand the mystery they contained. This is the teaching of Saint Augustine: "Thus Joseph was more a prophet — because he understood the meaning of the seven ears and the seven head of cattle — than Pharaoh, who saw these things in dreams. Pharaoh had a form imprinted on his mind so that he might see, but the mind of Joseph was enlightened so that he might understand. The former, therefore, had the gift of tongues, the latter the gift of prophecy, because the former possessed the image of things but the latter was able to interpret the images."[28] And, a little further on, "But most a prophet is he who excels in both respects, that is, who sees in his spirit the symbolic likenesses of things corporeal and understands them due to the vigor of the mind." All this should be kept in mind when dealing with the points that follow.

Page 111: "I seem even now to hear that music made by so many sweet voices." One of the signs that a revelation is true, or that a favor is truly from God, is the constancy with which it remains impressed upon the soul, since the imagination cannot be the source of so strong an impression. This teaching is rightly repeated at many points in the heavenly books of holy Mother Teresa of Jesus; see her *Life*, chapter 37.

Page 113: "It [the soul] is more beautiful in God's eyes than the sun." This holy Father combined charity and humility. Charity compelled him to regard the sins of others as his own and to ask God's forgiveness for them, as he says in Book III, Chapter 2: "O my King and my God, forgive me, Lord, for everything in which they fail to obey you and keep your holy law!" In like manner, his great humility causes him to refer in the third person, as it were, to the great beauty of his own soul, a beauty greater than that of the sun, as God showed him in this vision. So too the Apostle Paul, who was taught in the same school of the humble Christ, spoke of himself as though he were another: *I know a man . . . who was caught up to the third heaven* (2 Cor 12:2). This attitude was imitated by Saint Columba, an Irish hermit and folllower of the institute and rule which Saint Patrick followed when he told of secret revelations in a passage which I shall cite below. The holy Mother Teresa of Jesus speaks of her soul in like manner in her *Life.*[29]

Page 114: "My God . . . I shall never cease." In my opinion, this vision was not one of those which Saint Augustine calls "spiritual," not because they deal with spiritual things but because they deal with them through images that are present in the soul without the senses having produced them.[30] Although this vision may have originated in a spiritual vision of mountain, fire, and light, it belonged nonetheless by its nature among the highest intellectual visions, for the holy man says (page 114): "And in my dream I understood that your divinity fills the entire world." And, a little further on (page 115), "Sovereign Lord, you know what my soul saw in that intense light; what I know is that the delight my soul felt during that short time cannot be compared to anything created," and so on. In order to see that this vision was truly an intellectual one, compare what Saint Augustine says about himself: "I entered, and with the eye of my soul, such as it was, I saw the light that never changes casting its rays over the same eye of my soul, over my mind. It was not the common light of day that is seen by the eye of every living thing of flesh and blood, nor was it some more spacious light of the same sort, as if the light of day were to shine far, far brighter than it does and fill all space with a vast brilliance," and so on;[31] and, a little further on, "All this, my God, you are."[32] Compare it also with a similar passage in the last chapter of the *Life* of holy Mother Teresa.

Page 115: he says that the saints do not doubt that Saint Paul saw the divine essence in that ecstasy of his, for there are indeed some saints who hold this opinion: Saint Augustine,[33] Saint Anselm,[35] and Saint Thomas,[34] whom many theologians, past and present, have followed.

Page 115: "I was sleeping and did not have the use of my senses." The point which the holy man asserts here as certain is that whatever he saw he did not perceive it with the external senses, as he has already said quite clearly above. He does not say, however, whether he saw it through species already in the soul, received there from the senses on other occasions, or whether he saw it by means of new species given to the soul by God on this occasion. It may have happened either way, as Saint Thomas teaches,[36] but it is more appropriate in the present case that it happened in the second way, because this vision was, in my opinion, an intellectual vision, one that deals with objects which do not enter the soul through the senses (Saint Augustine has given an admirable explanation of this type of vision[37]). Master Fray Luis de Léon, a distinguished defender of the teaching of holy Mother Teresa of Jesus, has made the same point in connection with another of her visions in *The Interior Castle*.[38]

Page 116: "O my God and my Lord, how aptly your prophet David said in one of the psalms." The divine favor which the holy man reports in this section was by its nature an intellectual and very lofty vision, for he cites the words which Saint Augustine used in connection with another ecstasy of his own. The latter occurred while he was conversing with Monica, his mother, about the things of heaven: "Suppose that this state were to continue and all other visions of things inferior were to be removed, so that this single vision entranced and absorbed the one who beheld it and enveloped him in inward joys in such a way that for him life was eternally the same as that instant of understanding for which we had longed so much — would not this be what we are to understand by the words *Come and share the joy of your Lord*"?[39]

Page 116: "The grace of the Holy Spirit expands the soul, so that the more sweetness it receives, the larger it becomes and the more capable it is of that joy and sweetness." This is the specific effect of visions and favors when they are from God, as Saint Gregory teaches us in a splendid passage in which he is explaining how the glorious patriarch Saint Benedict could have seen the entire world in a single ray of light: "To the soul that sees the creator all of creation is cramped, for however little it glimpses of the light of the creator, everything created is now small in its eyes, since the innermost part of the mind is bathed in the light of the visions and is so enlarged in God that it is superior to the entire world — not that heaven and earth have in fact been reduced in size, but that the soul of the one who sees has been expanded."[40] The same light of the sovereign vision enlarges the heart so that in its view the entire world becomes exceedingly superfluous and seems but a crumb. Long before Saint Gregory, the same teaching was given to us by Saint Columba, who followed the institute and rule of Saint Patrick in Ireland. For Saint Adamnan, who wrote his biography, tells us how a disciple named Lugreus questioned him: "I wish you would tell me whether these prophetic revelations came to you through visions or locutions or in some manner unknown to other human beings." Once Columba had made him swear not to say anything to anyone as long as he, Columba, was still alive, he answered the question: "There are some, but very few, whose innermost minds God in his goodness enlarges to a marvelous degree and whom he allows to see the whole surface of the earth, as well as the seas and the heavens, with the utmost clarity, in a single moment, as though in the light of a single ray of the sun."

Page 120: In connection with the dream in which the holy man saw himself being lowered through the air from a high place to the earth, he says, "I began to say, my Lord, has this occurred so that I might understand the change I have undergone?" and so on. Here he seems to be in doubt about the meaning of the dream which God had sent him, but it must be observed that while God reveals mysterious things to his servants both in dreams and while they are awake, he does not always grant them an immediate understanding of the mystery. On the contrary, he may grant it gradually, as happened to Saint Peter when three times he saw a sheet being let down from heaven, filled with a variety of insects and animals; the sacred text says: "While Peter was doubting within himself what the vision meant." Regarding this, Denis the Carthusian offers this excellent remark: "In this vision the Holy Spirit did not teach Peter immediately and completely, whether directly or through an angel, but step by step and, to some extent, through other human beings, in order to maintain the human mind in humility. The same phenomenon can be seen in the visions given to Daniel, Ezekiel, and other prophets, to whom the mystery was not made known at the time the vision was given, so that the soul might be humbled by the darkness in which it found itself, and might exercise its own mental powers.

It will have struck some that in the *Confessions* of this holy man there is more about the favors and blessings which he received from the hand of God than about his own sins. If we look carefully, however, he does not fail to confess the sins which he admits he committed, as can be seen in Book I, Chapter 1 (page 39): "I resolved . . . to write down my sins in this book, after having often, by your grace, confessed them in the sacrament. I do so in order that, if any read them, they may praise your grace and mercy and also pray for me, a sinner." Elsewhere he confesses his ingratitude in view of the many great blessings he had received from God. Then, in Book I, Chapter 5 (page 46): "Sweet Jesus, salvation of my soul, how often I have offended you with my tongue, which you gave me that I might praise and thank you always!" In Book I, Chapter 7 (page 51): "My Glory, for the sake of that great humility forgive all my thoughtless arrogance."

In Book II, Chapter 9 (page 77), speaking of the vow of chastity, he says, "But the struggle against thoughts is usually persistent and dangerous; therefore to whatever extent I have failed to resist quickly and strongly (this is something you know better than I!), I accuse myself and am grieved; in your great mercy forgive me." In the same Book, Chapter 13 (page 85): "Lord, I do not deserve the noble name of human being, since I did not follow reason when I offended you who are worthy of being praised and adored by all your creatures as their Lord."

In Book III, Chapter 2 (page 91), he asks forgiveness for all the sins which others commit, as though he were himself guilty because others fail to obey the law of God. If we wonder at these few and slight sins, we should wonder even more at the efficacious grace of God that is able to preserve some souls in a state of purity, so that while they are not free of the venial sins into which human beings fall through inadvertence, they do indeed pass some period of their lives in freedom from such venial sins as spring from free will. Father Francisco Suarez says expressly, "If we restrict ourselves to deliberate venial sins, it is believable that some saints, for some periods of their lives, reached such a degree of perfection that they rarely or never committed such sins."[41]

I admit that the phenomena which marked the life of this great servant of God were indeed rare and exceptional. But as a worthy ancient writer of the life of the outstanding bishop and martyr Emmeram said, "In my opinion, if we are unable to imitate the actions of the saints, we may at least meditate on, at least admire, that which we would like to do, so that we may at some future time will to do what we admire. For the divine mercy is not bounded, but helps even where there are no merits."

NOTES

1. Saint Thomas, *Summa theologiae* 1, q. 12, a. 7 ad 1.
2. Council of Trent, Session VI, Chapter 7.
3. Saint Augustine, *The Magnitude of the Soul* 31, 77.
4. *Ibid.*, 31, 78.
5. Saint Augustine, *Homilies on the Gospel of John* 6, 15; 62, 3.
6. Alfonso Salmeron, *Tem. 12 in Novum Testamentum*, tract. 36.
7. Enriquez, *De ordinibus* X, 3 and 7.
8. Saint Thomas, *Summa theologiae* 22, q. 186, a. 2c and 9c.
9. Gregory of Valencia, *In 2-2 Summae theologiae*, disp. 10, cap. 4.
10. Saint Augustine, *Te Deum.*
11. Saint Peter Chrysologus, Sermon 48.
12. Saint Augustine, Sermon 12 on the Birth of Christ (*Opera*, vol. 17).
13. Abbot Guerric, Sermon 3 on the Annunciation, 4; among the works of Saint Bernard (ed. Mabillon) 6, 879.
14. Galen, *De sanitate tuenda*, Lib. I; Avicenna, Lib. I, sent. 3, doct.1, cap. 2.
15. Saint Thomas, *Summa theologiae* 3, q. 16, a. 5c.
16. Melchior Cano, *De locis theologicis* XII, 11.
17. Gregory of Valencia, *In tertiam partem*, disp. 1, q. 9, punct. 2.
18. Francisco Suárez, *In tertiam partem*, tom. 2, disp. 33, sect. 2.
19. Gabriel Vázquez, *In tertiam partem*, disp. 56, cap. 2.
20. Council of Trent, Session VI, chapter 16.
21. Saint Thomas, *Summa theologiae* 22, q. 174, a. 3c; see also a. 4c.
22. Saint Augustine, *The Literal Meaning of Genesis* 12, 12 and 18.
23. Saint Augustine, *Confessions* 12, 12.
24. Saint Gregory, *Dialogues* 4, 48.
25. Cardinal Torquemada, Preface 2.
26. Saint Thomas, *Summa theologiae* 22, q. 171, a. 5.
27. Saint John Chrysostom, *Prooemium in psalmos* 2; see also Saint Ambrose, *Commentary on Luke* 2; Saint Gregory, *Homilies on Ezekiel* 1 (near end).
28. Saint Augustine, *The Literal Meaning of Genesis* 12, 9.
29. Saint Teresa of Avila, *Life*, last chapter.
30. Saint Augustine, *The Literal Meaning of Genesis* 12, 67.

31. Saint Augustine, *Confessions* 7, 10, 1.

32. *Ibid.*, 7, 10, 2.

33. Saint Augustine, Letter 112, 12-13.

34. Saint Anselm, *In 2 Cor. 12.*

35. Saint Thomas, *Summa theologiae* 1, q. 12, a. 11 ad 2; 22, q. 174, a. 4; 22, q. 175, a. 3.

36. Saint Thomas, *Summa theologiae* 22, q. 174, a. 1 ad 3.

37. Saint Augustine, *The Literal Meaning of Genesis* 12, 67.

38. Luis de Léon, *Libro de las Moradas* 1.

39. Saint Augustine, *Confessions* 9, 10, 3.

40. Saint Gregory, *Dialogues* 2, 36.

41. Francisco Suarez, *De gratia*, tom. II, lib. 5, cap. 8, no. 2.

Blessed Alonso de Orozco

by J. M. Romero (Monastery of the Encarnación, Madrid)

The publication of the English translation
of the *Confesiones del Beato Alonso de Orozco*
commemorates the 400th anniversary
of Blessed Alonso's death

19 September 1591 — 1991